NEW EDITION!

Human BE-ing

How To Have A Better Relationship

Written
and
Illustrated
by

D0916255

William V. Pietsch

Trafford
PUBLISHING™

Note for Librarians: A cataloguing record for this book is available from Library and Archives
Canada at www.collectionscanada.ca/amicus/index-e.html
ISBN 1-55212-369-3

Printed in Victoria, BC, Canada. Printed on paper with minimum 30% recycled fibre.
Trafford's print shop runs on "green energy" from solar, wind and other environmentally-friendly power sources.

Offices in Canada, USA, Ireland and UK

Book sales for North America and international:
Trafford Publishing, 6E–2333 Government St.,
Victoria, BC V8T 4P4 CANADA
phone 250 383 6864 (toll-free 1 888 232 4444)
fax 250 383 6804; email to orders@trafford.com
Book sales in Europe:
Trafford Publishing (UK) Limited, 9 Park End Street, 2nd Floor
Oxford, UK OX1 1HH UNITED KINGDOM
phone +44 (0)1865 722 113 (local rate 0845 230 9601)
facsimile +44 (0)1865 722 868; info.uk@trafford.com
Order online at:
trafford.com/00-0033

10 9

"The best business managers go back to the basics again and again. This book is about some basics. Don't be deceived by its simple appearance; HUMAN BE-ING is a classic."

-James A. Vaughan, Ph.D.
Corporate consultant and co-author of Training in Industry

- How to break through the power struggle between two people, whether they are mates, family, friends, or coworkers.

- How to accept your emotions, good or bad, instead of letting others define how you should feel.

- How learning to love yourself frees you to love others.

- How to communicate effectively, and to listen to what others have to say.

Here at last is a guide that lets you identify your problems and see how to solve them.

This is a work of insight and understanding that will begin to help you from the opening pages to its final chapter.

DR. WILLIAM V. PIETSCH is a marriage and family therapist, and a consultant, writer, and lecturer on human relationships. He is a graduate of Northwestern University and Princeton Theological Seminary.

TABLE OF CONTENTS

TABLE OF CONTENTS (continued)

INTRODUCTION

The controls of a television set make it possible to enjoy the use of a very complicated instrument that we may not fully understand.

While occasionally problems arise in a TV set which need the work of a specialist, sometimes by consulting an instruction manual conditions can be greatly improved.

In our relationships as human beings, problems also arise which may require the help of a specialist. At other times, understanding some principles about ourselves can bring about much improvement.

This is an "instruction manual" about how to handle problems that come up in relationships.

BUT...WHERE TO BEGIN?

A relationship - like a jig-saw puzzle - can have many confusing parts to fit together.

With a jig-saw puzzle, however, there are **two basic steps** that make all the other steps that follow much simpler and easier:

1. We find pieces with the same color tone, and gather them together in groups:

2. And we find pieces with straight edges and create a corner or a frame of some sort:

While these two steps, in themselves, are not a final answer - if we **begin** with them, and **keep returning to them again and again** we move toward a solution.

Most people don't know that there are also **TWO KEY STEPS available for handling the problems we face in relationships.**

What makes these steps KEY steps is their focus on the two areas that are most basic in a relationship -
the feelings
over here

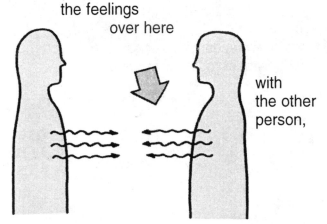

with
the other
person,

and the feelings we have
here within ourselves.

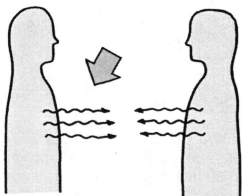

Once we get clear about what these two basic steps **are,** and **keep returning to them again and again**, the many parts of a relationship become much simpler and easier to fit together.

The TWO KEY STEPS in putting together a relationship are:

1. REFLECTING
and
2. PROTECTING

REFLECTING is what we do about the **other** person's feelings

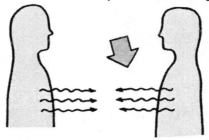

PROTECTING is what we do about our **own** feelings

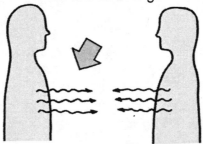

To understand REFLECTING in a relationship, it's useful to think of reflecting in the ordinary sense of that word:

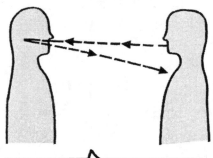

When a mirror reflects, it simply sends back what comes to it from "out there."

REFLECTING in a relationship does something similar:

The person reflecting listens to hear what the other person is saying, and then reflects back what has been heard.

YOU SEEM TO BE SAYING... is one example of

REFLECTING - letting the other person know that you are trying to hear what's being said.

Sensitive REFLECTING usually creates a change in the relationship in a very short time.

REFLECTING , however, is a skill that requires experience to do well. The details of how to go about it will be seen in the pages that follow.

There are, however, two key steps. What about the PROTECTING step?

Sometimes it's assumed that the only way to improve a relationship is to keep focusing on the other's needs, and not think about our own.

Yet, if we keep paying attention over here

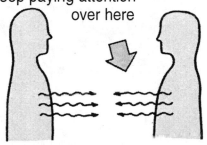

with the other person,

but remain completely silent about what's happening here, within ourselves,

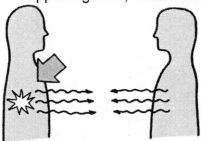

we will eventually develop an increasing resentment ("It's not fair!") creating problems for both ourselves and the other person.

PROTECTING is about taking care of our own feelings. It's about self respect. And courage to BE.

The specifics of how to use the two key steps
of REFLECTING and PROTECTING are available
in chapters 4 and 5.
 - In fact, you could read those two chapters
now, and apply what you've learned there to a
relationship, and you'd see results almost
immediately.

However, if you want a clearer picture of what's
happening beneath the surface in each person,
and how power struggles come about, it's vital
to read Chapters 1-3 about UNDERSTANDING
OURSELVES.

That section provides important background
information that will be very useful in developing
the skills of REFLECTING and PROTECTING.

As a consultant and psychotherapist I have
spent literally thousands of hours working
through relationship problems with people in
both personal and work situations.

My goal in this book is to share my experience
and some specific steps that you can use when
you face problems in relationships.

UNDERSTANDING OURSELVES

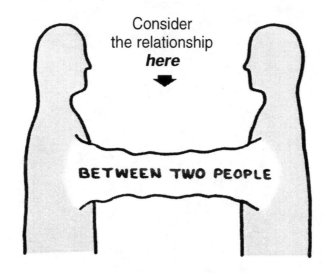

Consider
the relationship
here

BETWEEN TWO PEOPLE

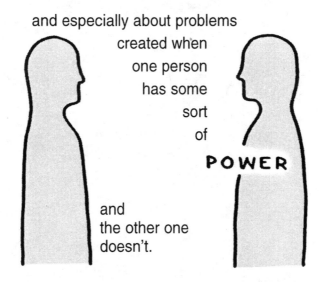

and especially about problems
created when
one person
has some
sort
of

POWER

and
the other one
doesn't.

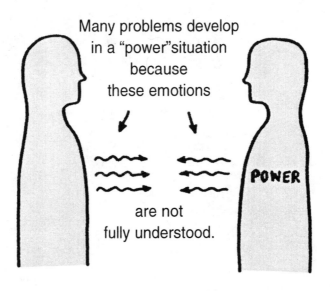

Many problems develop
in a "power" situation
because
these emotions

POWER

are not
fully understood.

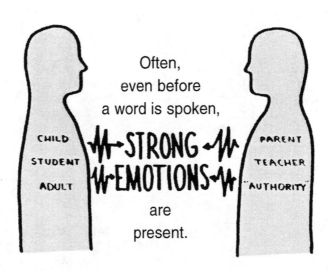

Often,
even before
a word is spoken,

CHILD
STUDENT
ADULT

STRONG
EMOTIONS

PARENT
TEACHER
"AUTHORITY"

are
present.

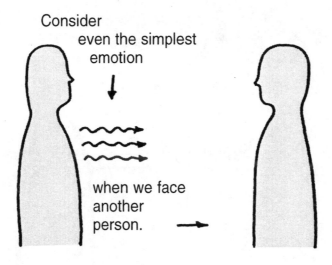

Consider even the simplest emotion

when we face another person.

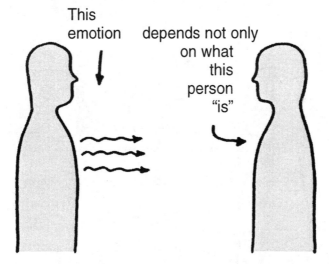

This emotion depends not only on what this person "is"

but also depends on . . .

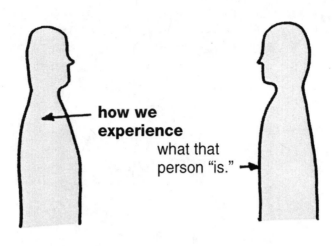

how we
experience
what that
person "is."

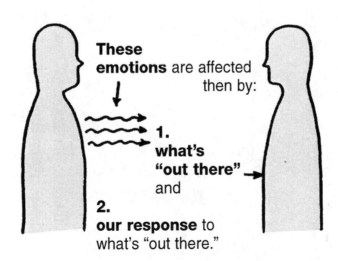

These
emotions are affected
then by:

1.
what's
"out there"
and

2.
our response to
what's "out there."

A major reason for problems
in our personal relationships
is that

WE SEE

WHAT WE

EXPECT TO SEE

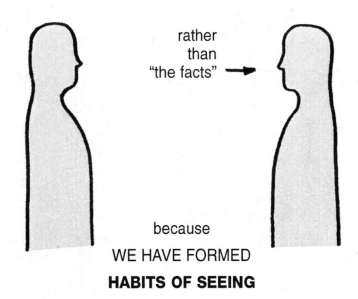

rather
than
"the facts" ➜

because

WE HAVE FORMED

HABITS OF SEEING

For example:

Do you see anything unusual about the above statement?

Look again.

If it still looks all right to you read it once more
. . . carefully.

Did you notice the second "A"?

Almost everybody gets it wrong at first.
Why? - Because we have a habit of seeing what we expect to see.

We give the phrase a "meaning" based on our past experience and leave out anything that doesn't fit in with that meaning.

So also . . .

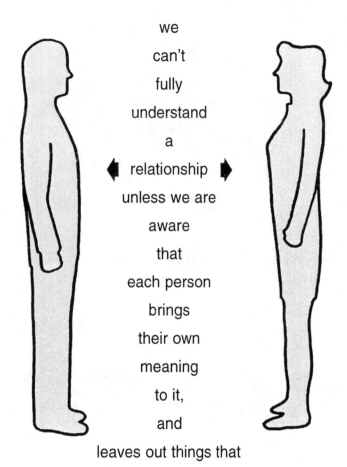

we
can't
fully
understand
a
◀ relationship ▶
unless we are
aware
that
each person
brings
their own
meaning
to it,
and
leaves out things that
don't fit in with that meaning.

Chapter 1

TRANSFERENCE AND POWER STRUGGLES

We all tend to look for a *"familiar type"* in persons we meet — and to leave out those qualities we don't expect in "that type."

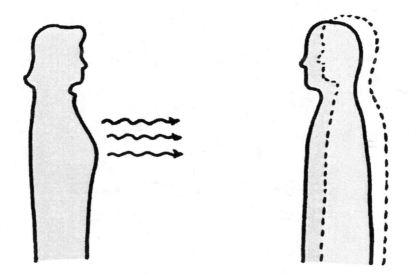

WITHOUT BEING AWARE OF IT
we may *transfer* to another person
emotions and *responses*
we once had towards someone else.

This process is appropriately called
"TRANSFERENCE."

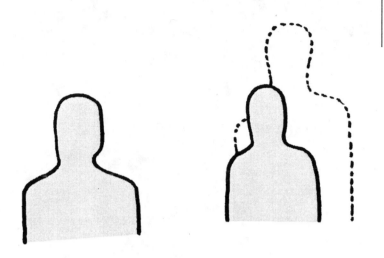

Even rather minor details might cause us to have transference to another person.

. . . For example, facing **another person who is sitting behind a desk** may make us feel inferior . . . or cause us to see the person as having abilities they may or may not have.

. . . Or if **the other person reminds us of someone we admire,** we may be less critical of that person than of someone else.

. . . Or we may see **a large quiet person** as being critical of us when that may not be true at all.

"Transference" occurs because

the human mind works

much like

a computer,

in which

"automatic

responses"

are

stored

away

for use

as needed . . .

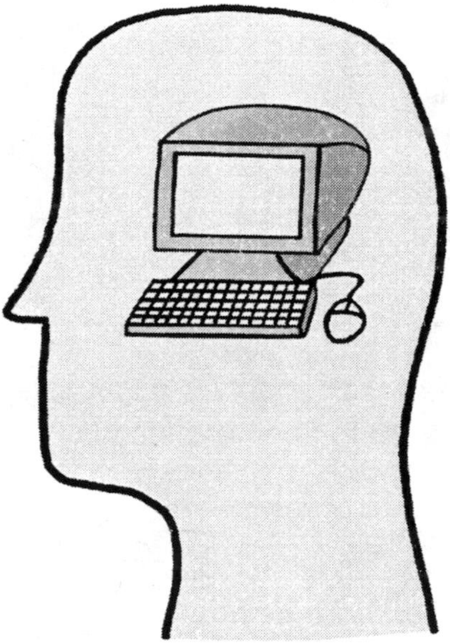

We make our actions "automatic"

so that we no longer have to repeat

"thinking through the details."

For example . . .

In *learning to drive a car*
  we must first think
  of each part individually

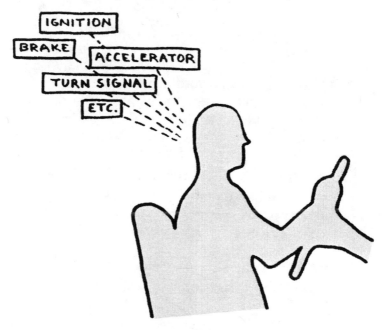

. . . but once these things are
"programmed" into our minds,
we are free to think about
other things:
  traffic patterns,
    road signs,
      weather conditions,

We learn to relate to the car
automatically, **"UNCONSCIOUSLY."**

In a similar way we relate
to other activities in AUTOMATIC or
"UNCONSCIOUS" ways:

In writing
we don't have to
keep thinking about
how to form each letter
and word; we concentrate on
the ideas and the writing comes
to us "automatically."

IN READING, words trigger certain automatic thoughts in our memories because we have trained our minds to respond in a certain way.

IN EATING,
our attention tends to
focus on the taste, rather
than on how to lift food to
our mouth, and how to
chew and swallow it.

We have programmed ourselves in thousands of ways . . . created habits to make life easier . . . so that we no longer have to think about **HOW** to do these things.

In summary, then, our "unconscious mind" serves a useful purpose, (freeing the conscious mind for other tasks), but it also creates problems in our relationships through

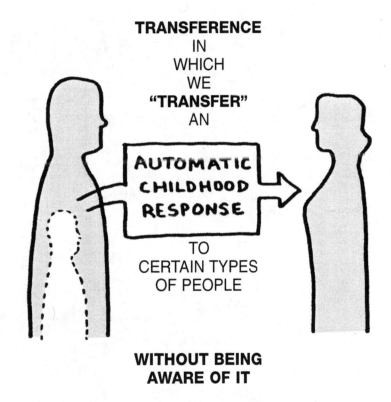

TRANSFERENCE
IN
WHICH
WE
"TRANSFER"
AN

AUTOMATIC CHILDHOOD RESPONSE

TO
CERTAIN TYPES
OF PEOPLE

**WITHOUT BEING
AWARE OF IT**

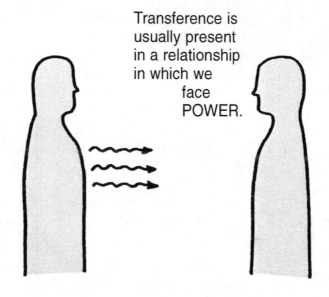

Transference is
usually present
in a relationship
in which we
face
POWER.

Such a situation often brings back
CHILDHOOD EMOTIONS
such as

"a sense of futility"
and
"a longing
to be the
one in power."

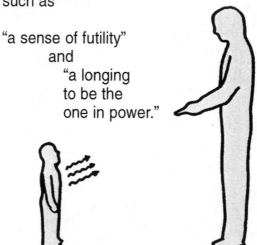

For years,
as children,
we lived
in an
inferior
position
to other
people
who had . . .

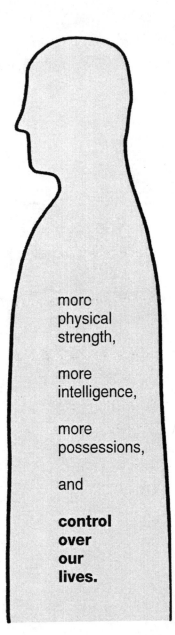

more
physical
strength,

more
intelligence,

more
possessions,

and

**control
over
our
lives.**

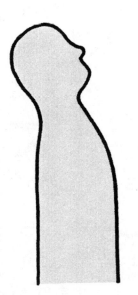

Gradually we figured out the best ways to
deal with those big people who had the power.

When we face power as adults, we tend to use those ways of relating that worked well in the past.

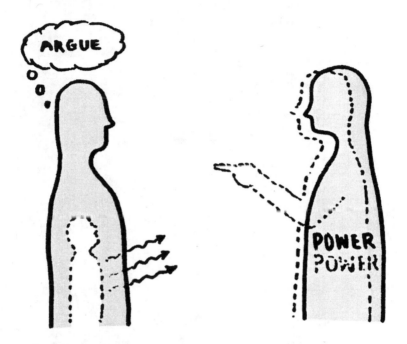

Transferring childhood responses to another adult is most likely when we feel "weak," "tired," or "under pressure."

An awareness of TRANSFERENCE provides a key to understanding both ourselves and others in almost every human relationship.

A simplified, but specific example of
how transference comes about
can be seen
in a relationship
where
a
person
faced
a
situation of
"constant pressure"
as a
child.

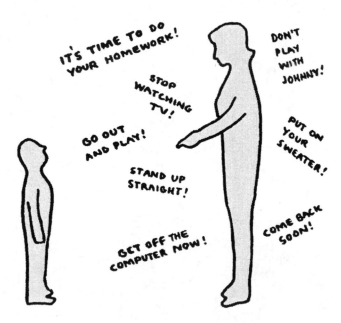

If we had an **over demanding parent**, we probably tried to handle it in various ways as a child:

For example . . .
we might have tried to
"BE GOOD"

I'LL DO IT RIGHT AWAY!

. . . but such a
"way of relating"
had a problem . . .

our time would be given over to what the parent wanted, which wouldn't leave much time for ourselves.

On the other hand . . .
    to **REBEL**
    also had its
    problems. To say . . .

I WON'T DO IT! AND YOU CAN'T MAKE ME !

. . . would have caused that powerful parent (who controlled TV, ice cream, etc.) to withhold those things we wanted.

The most effective method of relating to an over demanding parent was often **DELAY**.

"I'll do it" — gained parent's approval
". . . LATER" — gained time for ourselves.

Once "the best way of relating" was discovered, we tended to program the *automatic response* that most easily fit that type of relationship:

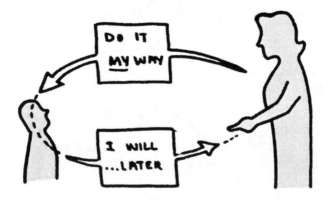

Throughout life we tend to repeat the most effective ways of relating when we face similar situations:

Of course, sometimes delays are very necessary. However, if every demand produces a delay, then transference is probably present.

ANOTHER EXAMPLE OF
how transference comes about
can be seen in a relationship

in
which
a
person
had a
background
where people
QUICKLY
RESPONDED
TO HIS NEEDS.

When we have had such a childhood we tend to be impatient as adults, but also "spontaneous" and "charming" because we didn't have a constant struggle to get power.

Childhood struggles would only occur when the parent "reached the limit" and refused to "give in."

At that point
a "temper tantrum"
or an accusation
"You don't love me"

was probably
very effective
in regaining
power.

If we had parents who "gave in" easily, we are likely to interpret even reasonable needs of another as proof that the other "does not care." We may not see ourselves as acting in self-centered and impulsive ways.

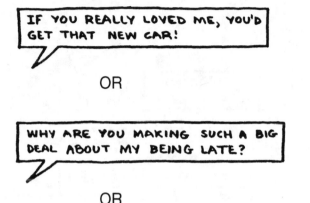

IF YOU REALLY LOVED ME, YOU'D GET THAT NEW CAR!

OR

WHY ARE YOU MAKING SUCH A BIG DEAL ABOUT MY BEING LATE?

OR

WHY DO WE HAVE TO DO IT YOUR WAY?

Surprisingly, people who have had parents who were "easy" on them may sometimes be attracted to persons who are demanding because such persons seem to provide a structure that was missing in childhood. The person with an over demanding parent in childhood my be attracted to a person who seems "spontaneous" and less rigid.

Most commonly, however, without realizing it, we repeat the familiar patterns of childhood.

Power struggles come about most vividly when each person has transference to the other, and uses "seemingly logical" but childish maneuvers in a power situation:

WHAT
THEN,
CAN
WE
DO
ABOUT
IT?

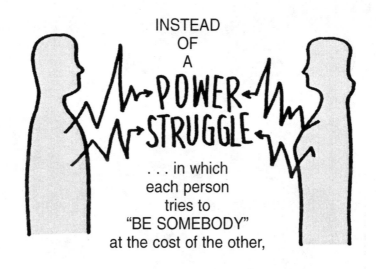

INSTEAD
OF
A
POWER
STRUGGLE
. . . in which
each person
tries to
"BE SOMEBODY"
at the cost of the other,

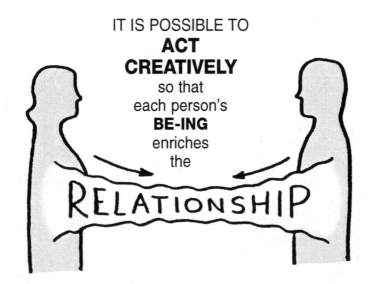

IT IS POSSIBLE TO
**ACT
CREATIVELY**
so that
each person's
BE-ING
enriches
the

RELATIONSHIP

Although we human beings are much alike,
among the billions of people in the world,
no two of us are identical. (Not even
"identical" twins!)

Each person has something unique to offer to the
rest of us . . .
. . . a new method of doing something
    . . . a fact
        . . . an experience
            . . . an insight into the meaning
            of grief or joy . . .

That uniqueness comes forth and enriches the life of
each person in a CREATIVE RELATIONSHIP.

"TO CREATE"

means

"to bring into BE-ing."

A
CREATIVE
RELATIONSHIP

is

a

RELATIONSHIP

where

each person's

UNIQUENESS

comes

into

BE-ING

and

enriches the other.

HOW THEN
DO WE DEVELOP
A
CREATIVE
RELATIONSHIP?

We move away from a power struggle and toward a creative relationship when we:

1. TRUST that there is a basic healthy drive deep within each person.   pg 48

2. PROVIDE conditions that make it easy for a person to BE somebody emotionally.   pg 64

3. REFLECT back what we are hearing through
TRUSTING
LISTENING and
CLARIFYING.   pg 76

4. PROTECT our own "self" through
DEFINING and
DEFENDING territory.   pg 134

5. EXPLORE alternatives with "self" respect.   pg 166

6. RISK a change in our own position.   pg 183

Chapter 2

THE PROBLEM
OF TRUST

We act creatively in a
"power" situation when we

TRUST

that

deep within each person

there is a healthy drive

toward

what is seen as

good and right

At times it is difficult to understand how we could trust in any sort of basic goodness in another human being.

Such feelings are quite understandable in light of some of the things we see in "human nature."

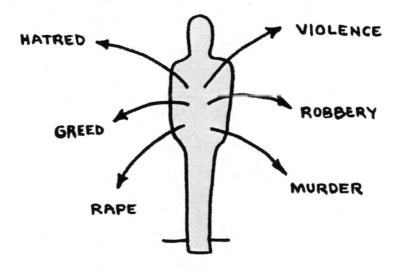

It seems that a person's basic inner nature is filled with destructive desires seeking to escape.

Some religious institutions and
some psychological viewpoints see
basic human nature as
"VOLCANIC"
with

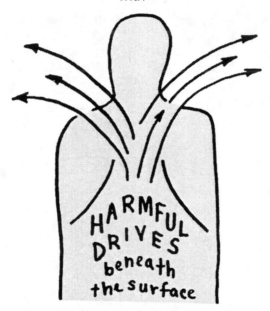

which must be
controlled by
moral "law" and "discipline"
or always "channeled" by ego control.

Such an ***emphasis*** is a
MISUNDERSTANDING
OF THE
BASIC NATURE OF A HUMAN BEING.

Rather than being "VOLCANIC"
(filled with unorganized drives)
HUMAN BEINGS ARE BASICALLY

"ORGANIC"

*. . . Systematically moving toward
wholeness.*

Just as a seed for a plant, or a tree, somehow
"knows" what it will someday become, so also,
**human beings have within them a sense of
"purpose"** — a "knowledge" of what they are
intended to be.

Just as this

"knowledge"

of

"POTENTIAL

MATURITY"

exists

within

a

SEED,

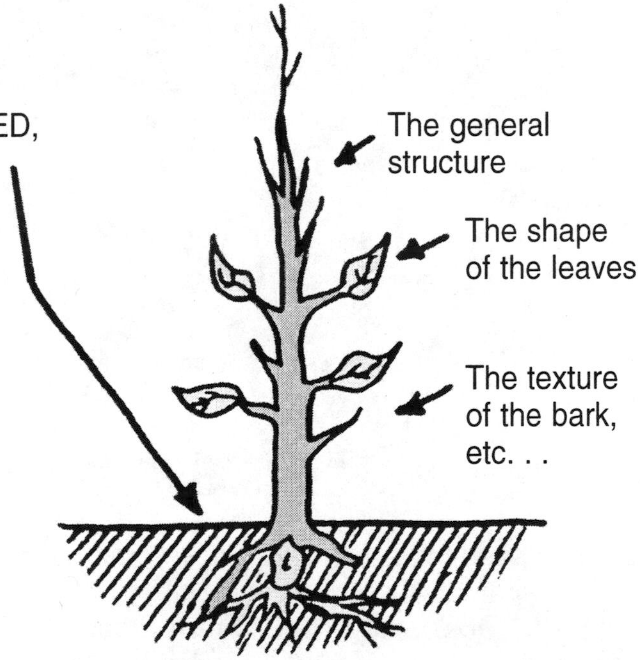

The general
structure

The shape
of the leaves

The texture
of the bark,
etc. . .

so also . . .

. . . a knowledge* of

POTENTIAL MATURITY

exists

within a

HUMAN BEING

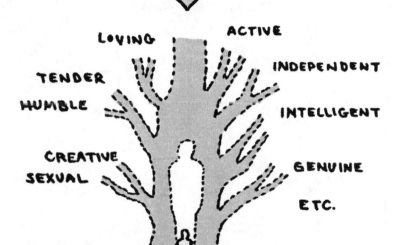

*Known, but not necessarily clearly defined. "The author who benefits you most is not the one who tells you something you did not know before, but the one who gives expression to the truth that has been struggling in you for utterance."

— Oswald Chambers

But . . . if a person is

ORGANIC

and potentially "good,"

how can we explain

"HARMFUL DRIVES"?

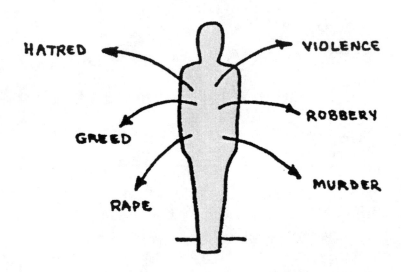

What seem like "harmful drives"
are actually the result of

CUTTING OFF GROWTH

in much the same way that
a tree is pruned:

While a
mature tree
might look
something
like this ▶

If too many
branches are
cut off

here

. . . there may be
so much growth
here

that the tree ends up
"OUT OF BALANCE."

Ideally, we might see our
POTENTIAL MATURITY
as something like this:

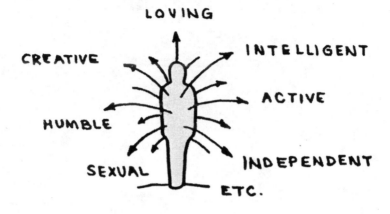

If certain
"branches" of
the personality
are not allowed
to grow,
however . . .

other characteristics
**get out of proportion
to the rest:**

ACTIVE

INDEPENDENT

... while being

ACTIVE
and
INDEPENDENT

are *good qualities*
in themselves . . .

. . . such characteristics
not balanced

by a similar
maturity
here

(in love,
tenderness,
humility,
sexuality,
etc.)

. . . means problems
may be created
here

ACTIVE

INDEPENDENT

VIOLENCE   GREED   RAPE

Or if

TENDERNESS
and
HUMILITY

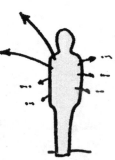

get
"OUT OF PROPORTION"

and are **not balanced by active independent qualities**

Other kinds of problems may occur:

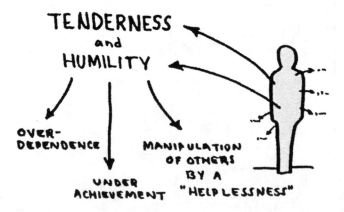

TENDERNESS
and
HUMILITY

OVER-
DEPENDENCE

UNDER
ACHIEVEMENT

MANIPULATION
OF OTHERS
BY A
"HELPLESSNESS"

In daily life, persons with

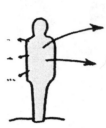

ACTIVE
and
INDEPENDENT qualities

(not balanced by other,
more passive ones),
might express themselves
in such attitudes as:

> IF YOU DON'T TAKE CARE OF
> YOURSELF, NO ONE ELSE WILL!

> NOBODY PUSHES ME AROUND!

> I'M NOT A CRY BABY LIKE OTHER PEOPLE!

While an overemphasis

on **TENDERNESS**
and
HUMILITY

might result in

> WILL YOU HELP ME? I CAN NEVER DO
> ANYTHING RIGHT!

or

> WHATEVER YOU SAY IS ALL RIGHT.

or

>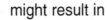

(the silent one)

We get "out of proportion" as human beings because we have been taught that it is **"wrong"** to have certain emotions:

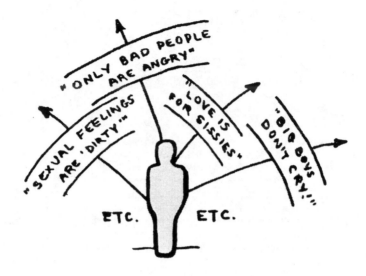

. . . and so eventually we
learn to hold back growth
in certain branches of our personality
because growth in
these areas seems
either ***futile*** or
too painful.

When we were children we often blamed ourselves for **having** certain emotions:

While the mature person does **not act on every emotion,** he or she does try to *accept* every emotion as part of his or her **be-ing.**

Once we understand that every emotion that we have "makes sense" someplace within us, based on what seemed true in the past, then

ACCEPTING
a
PRESENT EXPERIENCE
of
THAT EMOTION

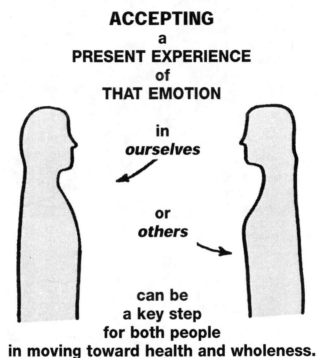

in
ourselves

or
others

can be
a key step
for both people
in moving toward health and wholeness.

Even if we don't understand why we are experiencing a certain emotion, accepting that experience as part of our "self," or accepting another's experience as part of that person's "self," usually brings about a growth toward maturity.

Chapter 3

THE NEED
TO BE SOMEBODY

We also act creatively in
a "power" situation
when we

PROVIDE

CONDITIONS

that make it easy

for a person

to

BE SOMEBODY

EMOTIONALLY

It is certainly understandable that "accepting emotions" may seem, at first, to be a dangerous step to take.

Perhaps if emotions are not "held back," they could keep on escalating to a point of destructive action.

In reality, pushing back emotional energy usually causes that energy to become more and more forceful as it seeks to express itself.

Practically speaking, in an argument when the other person has strong feelings . . .

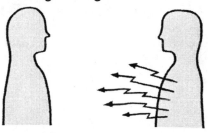

if we keep explaining that

YOU SHOULDN'T FEEL THAT WAY!

. . . then, those feelings, instead of becoming less, will usually become stronger.

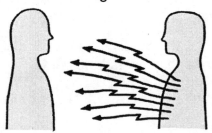

Unfortunately, in dealing with human emotions, we often put the emphasis on "getting things back in shape" by using FORCE (discipline, "law and order," etc.) on those areas of "trouble"

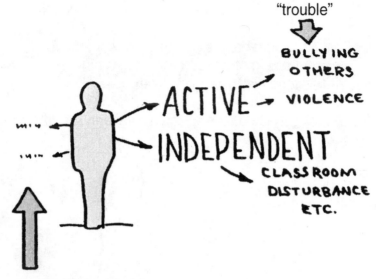

ACTIVE → BULLYING OTHERS

→ VIOLENCE

INDEPENDENT

↘ CLASSROOM DISTURBANCE ETC.

. . . rather than by providing conditions for growth here to bring about a **balance** in emotions.

FORCE (while sometimes helpful), **usually deals ONLY WITH SYMPTOMS . . . NOT THE SOURCE OF THE PROBLEM.**

Generally speaking, problems come about **not because** we were not allowed to **do** something, but because we not allowed to **BE** somebody.

If the **source** of human problems is found in the fact that we were kept from BEING (certain emotions were not acceptable)

. . . the **solution** is found in providing conditions so that emotional growth, which once seemed futile or too painful, can begin again . . .

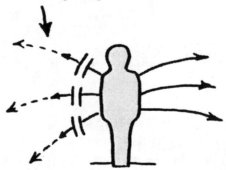

. . . so the person can move toward being "whole."

Unfortunately, WELL-MEANING adults, who were worried about *"harmful drives"* attempted to "MOLD US INTO SHAPE" because they feared **human BE-ING**. Such pressure, instead of solving human problems, actually **CREATED THEM!**

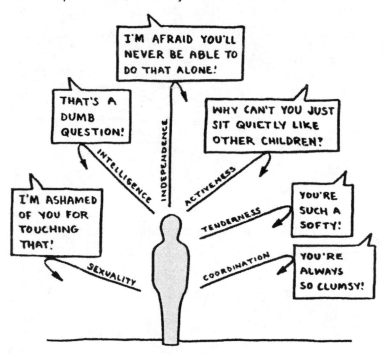

While all of us have probably heard some version of the above words, it is not the occasional comments which affect us, but rather it is those phrases which are repeated over and over again (Perhaps to our-selves!) which eventually keep us from growing in certain areas.

The effect of pressure on emotions might be made clearer if we think of emotions as being like air in a child's balloon.

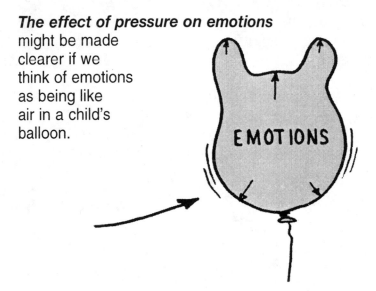

Certain areas get "out-of-proportion"

when **_other areas_** are **_"held in."_**

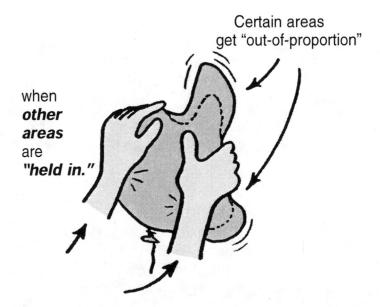

Emotions which are continually
"held in" by a parent
here

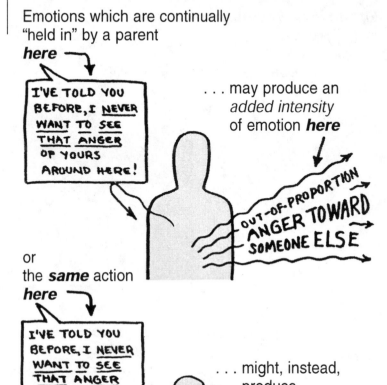

I'VE TOLD YOU BEFORE, I NEVER WANT TO SEE THAT ANGER OF YOURS AROUND HERE!

. . . may produce an *added intensity* of emotion **here**

OUT-OF-PROPORTION ANGER TOWARD SOMEONE ELSE

or
the **same** action
here

I'VE TOLD YOU BEFORE, I NEVER WANT TO SEE THAT ANGER OF YOURS AROUND HERE!

. . . might, instead, produce

UNREALISTIC FEAR OF OTHERS

. . . while it may not be possible to predict
how a person will respond when "held in"
in a certain area, the need to **BE** is always
present — seeking some form of expression.

. . . just as water from a hose when held back

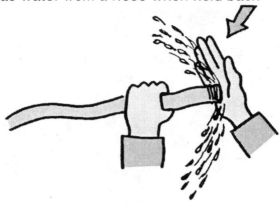

finds another way of escape, persons who are
kept from **BE-ING** in certain ways will find
another way to BE.

If,   as adults we will
as a child,   then seek *another*
being tender   way of **BE-ING**
produced   that brings *rewards*
ridicule . . .   without tenderness

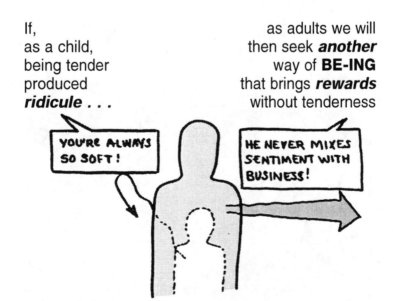

. . . what is needed in a balloon
to "get things back in shape"
is not more pressure on
the areas "out of proportion"

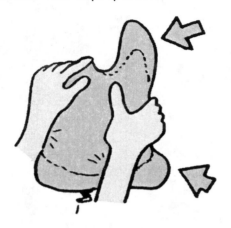

but a RELEASE OF PRESSURE
on the areas "held in"

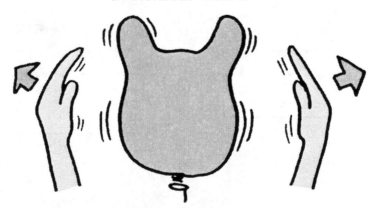

so that it can be
what it was created to be.

So also with human beings . . . what is needed for a person to become what he or she is intended to be — to grow into maturity — is **not more pressure** on the areas that are out-of-proportion . . .

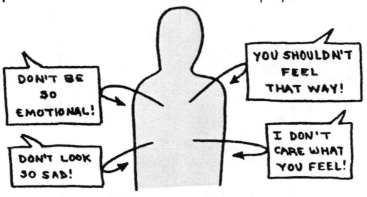

but a **release of pressure**
on the areas "held in"

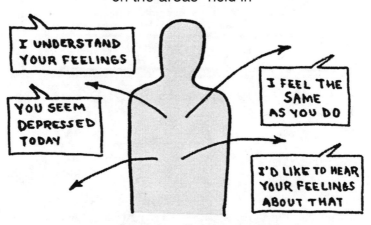

so the person can
BE SOMEBODY EMOTIONALLY.

It's important to be clear, however, that accepting emotions in another person - or even in ourselves - does not mean that anything a person DOES is completely acceptable.

In the real world of relationships there are times when aggressive stubborn people take actions with little or no regard for the needs of others. And sometimes even caring and sincere people may hurt others without knowing it.

Whatever the source, what to do about hurtful actions is a basic problem in relationships.

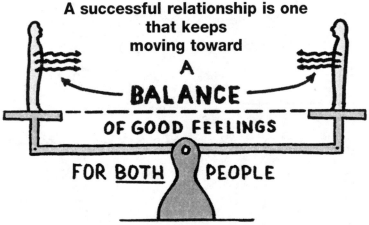

A successful relationship is one that keeps moving toward

A

BALANCE

OF GOOD FEELINGS

FOR BOTH PEOPLE

While REFLECTING an understanding of another's feelings is usually the best place to begin in improving a relationship, in any continuing relationship PROTECTING is also needed. In PROTECTING we demonstrate the healthy need to take care of ourselves as well as the other person.

USING THE TWO KEY STEPS

Chapter 4

REFLECTING

If we want to improve a relationship the best place to begin is **REFLECTING**

. . . REFLECTING BACK
UNDERSTANDING
OF THE OTHER
PERSON'S MESSAGE

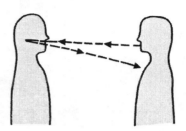

This is more than simply reflecting back the words that have been spoken. It's about trying to hear and understand what the other person is feeling, and then "checking it out" to see if we've heard correctly.

Once the other person senses that we are trying to understand, the relationship usually begins to improve.

This kind of understanding includes

TRUSTING
LISTENING and
CLARIFYING

Sometimes we take these three steps almost intuitively, but for sensitive reflecting in a growing relationship, we need to understand their deeper meaning.

TRUSTING depends more on what we **are** (our personal viewpoint) than on something we "DO."

Trust is more likely when we understand that another person

1. May be using **unconscious patterns** in relating to us.

2. Is not basically against us, but **simply trying to BE somebody emotionally**.

(**As described in the previous section:** UNDERSTANDING OURSELVES.)

But

TRUSTING ALSO MEANS

A CONSCIOUS

EFFORT TO

<u>WITHHOLD</u>

<u>JUDGMENT</u>

WHY a person *has a certain emotion* at a particular time is the result of *many past experiences*

. . . so that no one has a right to arrogantly inform another: **"You shouldn't feel that way!"**

An emotion is not what another person is deliberately "doing" to us, but simply what a person "HAS" at a particular moment.

We sometimes quickly PRE-JUDGE a person by **actions alone** without the slightest thought of what might be behind the action.

While our judgment of the person's motive *might* be accurate, to evaluate all the conscious and unconscious motives behind an act (even in our own lives!) is extremely complicated.

Many broken relationships have come about (some of them lasting for years) because, instead of withholding judgment, a person has judged another by actions alone.

While it may be necessary to evaluate a certain action

IT'S WRONG TO STEAL

. . . and prevent it from happening,

. . . it is quite another matter to evaluate another's WORTH AS A HUMAN BEING

I'M A FAR BETTER PERSON THAN HE IS, BECAUSE I WOULD NEVER DO THAT!

. . . perhaps with a similar personal history our own actions might even be worse than those of the other person.

It is important to separate the TWO ways of judging another person:

**the
ACTION**

**and the person's
BE-ING**

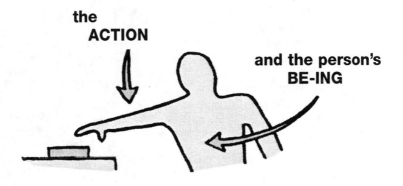

Evaluating an action:

> THAT'S NOT RIGHT, AND I WON'T ALLOW HIM TO DO THAT TO ME!

. . . while important
and necessary,
is **not the same** as
evaluating a person:

> ANY PERSON WHO _DOES THAT_ IS _NO GOOD!_

Examples of withholding judgment in typical situations:

> I'M NOT CLEAR WHY HE'S ANGRY.
> I WONDER IF HE HAS SOME SORT OF
> TRANSFERENCE TO ME...I'D BETTER
> TAKE A LOOK AT MYSELF TOO......
> I MAY HAVE TRANFERENCE TO HIM!

> HIS PUSHY ATTITUDE GETS TO ME!
> HE MUST FEEL INSECURE AND FEEL
> HE HAS TO BE SOMEBODY IN THIS
> SITUATION......THAT SOUNDS RATHER
> SMUG OF ME... HUH!... AND I WAS
> DOING THE SAME THING HE DID - JUST
> YESTERDAY - ... THAT'S INTERESTING!

> WHAT HE'S DOING SEEMS DOWNRIGHT
> CRUEL TO ME! - I WONDER IF SOMEONE
> TREATED HIM LIKE THAT WHEN HE WAS
> A KID!....IN ANY CASE, I OUGHT TO
> HEAR HIM OUT...... I MIGHT LEARN
> SOMETHING ABOUT MYSELF!

Such withholding of judgment can be
the first step in changing the direction
of a relationship.

In thinking about how relationships change, consider the physical law of inertia, which tells us that things tend to continue as they are:

A wheel
spinning
in this
direction

. . . tends to
keep going
that way

And a wheel
spinning in
the
opposite
direction

. . . tends to
continue
that way.

Once moving, ***a slight push*** in the same direction, from either person, ***keeps it moving***

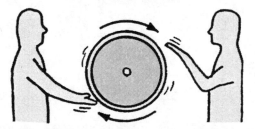

If each continues to push in this way, stopping soon becomes very difficult.

In the world of relationships there seems to be a law of **"emotional inertia"** in which things tend to continue as they are . . .

Once moving in a particular direction a "slight push" from either person will keep things moving in the same direction.

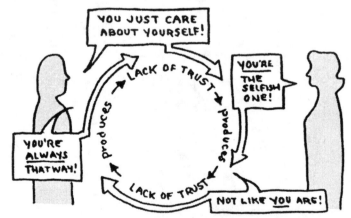

If each continues to "push" in this way, stopping soon becomes extremely difficult, and the chance of reversing the cycle is very unlikely.

BY WITHHOLDING JUDGMENT,

. . . making the conscious decision
not to act on limited evidence,
we are, in a sense,
"NOT PUSHING."

While this may not
reverse the cycle,it may
at least permit it to slow down
so that reversing
may later become possible.

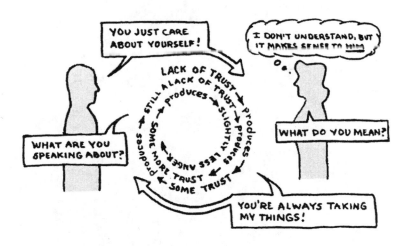

. . . Once a withholding of judgment
is sensed by the other person,
a new atmosphere is present
which prepares the way for an
for an increasingly creative relationship.

TRUSTING, then,

means being **aware**

that

1. **_Unconscious patterns_** are present in the relationship in **_both_** persons.

2. What seems to be an attack is often the other's **_attempt to BE somebody emotionally._**

3. Growth in the relationship may require a **_conscious effort to withhold judgment_** as to "why" the person feels as they do.

In addition to **T**RUSTING, *another condition that makes it easy for persons to BE who they are*
IS

LISTENING

Real Listening means "tuning in" to what the other person is *feeling* . . .

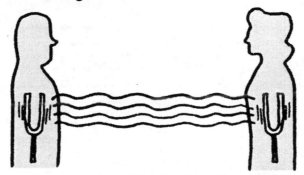

. . . so that we *listen to emotions*, not simply hear "ideas."

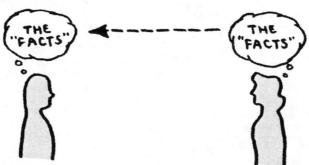

LISTENING means trying to "hear" the "deeper message" of the emotions:

such as

IT'S ELEVEN O'CLOCK AND HE'S NOT HERE YET.

SHE SEEMS WORRIED THAT HE'S LATE.

I'VE REALLY HAD IT WITH JOHN!

SHE'S ANGRY AND FRUSTRATED WITH JOHN.

SUZIE ALWAYS GETS WHAT SHE WANTS!

HE FEELS HE'S NOT TREATED FAIRLY.

WELL, ANOTHER WASTED DAY, AS USUAL.

HE SOUNDS DEPRESSED.

I NOTICE YOU HAD TIME TO DO WHAT YOU WANT!

SHE'S ANGRY WITH ME

Most of us have been trained to listen to "facts" rather than "feelings."

Actually, human beings are in **"stereo"** . . .

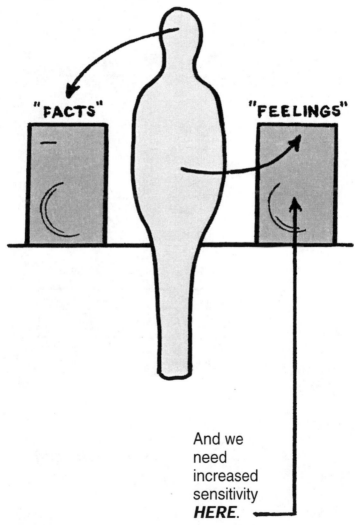

"FACTS"

"FEELINGS"

And we need increased sensitivity *HERE*.

Sometimes the message communicated by the emotions (through tone and physical expression), is the **complete reverse** or what is said through the **words:**

is

quite

a

different

message than:

. . . even though exactly the same words are used.

. . . may be a way of
sending **two messages**
at the same time . . .

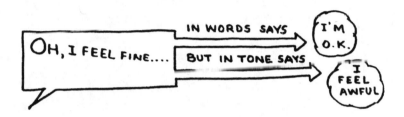

The double message "checks out"
(perhaps unconsciously) the other
person's depth of listening . . .
to see if he or she cares enough
to *really* hear what is being said.

**The person who LISTENS to the emotional
message demonstrates that he or she is
concerned about our BE-ING, and that helps
us to become more "whole."**

MOST OF US FIND IT DIFFICULT TO
listen to emotions.

Unfortunately, our formal education
has been
almost entirely
HERE

. . . and almost none
of it *HERE*

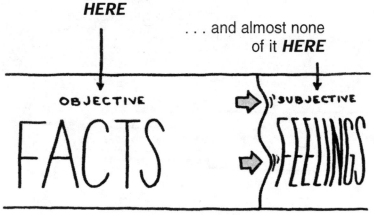

OBJECTIVE 'SUBJECTIVE

FACTS FEELINGS

. . . and we tend to solve problems the
way we were educated to solve them . . .
with the

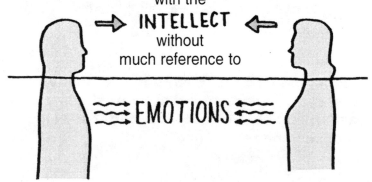

INTELLECT
without
much reference to

EMOTIONS

Actually, facts and feelings are not so easily separated. If strong emotions are ignored, communicating **"THE FACTS"** becomes *increasingly difficult:*

Sometimes very intense POWER STRUGGLES occur over issues that seem to be rather trivial:

On a deeper level, it is *not the action* which is taken that is really important, but *what the action means emotionally to each person:*

Arguments over trivials may really be saying . . .

The message of many arguments
(. . . if only we could hear it!)
is
"I WANT TO BE IMPORTANT TO YOU."

POWER STRUGGLES often end with remarks
such as

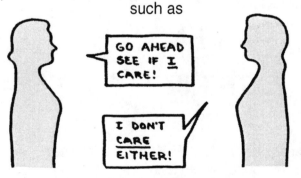

. . . which, interestingly, speaks
not about the "facts,"
but about the **relationship**.

A CREATIVE RELATIONSHIP in which growth is possible occurs when there is . . .

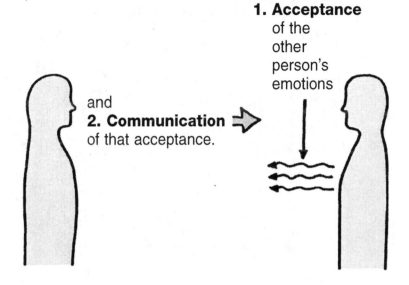

1. Acceptance
of the
other
person's
emotions

and
2. Communication
of that acceptance.

1. Acceptance of the other person's emotions
comes about through

TRUSTING
and
LISTENING

2. Communication of that acceptance
comes about through

CLARIFYING
— making clear to the other person
what has been heard.

To **CLARIFY** is helpful to

the listener

because

WHAT IS MEANT

may be
heard
as

SOMETHING ELSE

and *making clear what "facts" have been heard can prevent misunderstandings.*

> **BUT . . .**
>
> *the greatest value*
>
> *of* **CLARIFYING**
>
> **IS . . .**

. . . that it lets **the speaker**

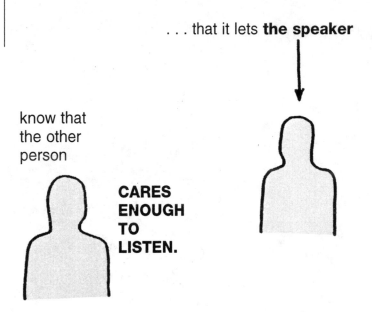

know that
the other
person

**CARES
ENOUGH
TO
LISTEN.**

It is not enough to say:

I UNDERSTAND.

We must **demonstrate that we understand by making clear WHAT has been heard:**

IT SOUNDS AS IF YOU ARE VERY HURT
ABOUT WHAT I HAVE DONE.

We demonstrate that we care enough to listen when we "tune in," not simply to the "factual" message . . .

. . . but to
the "deeper message"
of the *emotions*

When a person has strong emotions,
making clear that we have heard the
"factual" message...

I HEAR YOU SAYING THAT YOU'RE
GOING TO THE HOSPITAL.

is not of much value . . .
but making clear that the **PERSON**
has been heard . . .

YOU SOUND CONCERNED ABOUT IT.

is *tremendously helpful.*

CLARIFYING then, means *making clear to another person that the deeper message of the emotions has been heard.*

IT'S ELEVEN O'CLOCK AND HE'S NOT HERE YET.

SHE SEEMS WORRIED THAT HE'S LATE

YOU SOUND UNEASY ABOUT IT.

I'VE REALLY HAD IT WITH JOHN!

SHE'S ANGRY AND FRUSTRATED WITH HIM

IT SOUNDS AS IF YOU'VE REACHED YOUR LIMIT WITH JOHN!

SUZIE ALWAYS GETS WHAT SHE WANTS!

HE FEELS HE'S NOT BEING TREATED FAIRLY.

YOU FEEL SHE GETS MORE THAN YOU DO!

Clarifying does ***not*** mean
"I agree with your opinion"
but rather:

"I HEAR YOU SAYING . . ."

NOTE: Sincerity in trying to listen is vital. If the listener
is just "using a technique" (clarifying without trust and
listening) the other person will probably feel manipulated
and angry. Paraphrasing - rather than parroting - helps
the other person know that real understanding is there.

Unfortunately . . .

when there are strong emotions
in another person, we tend to feel
that the best way to deal with
the situation
is

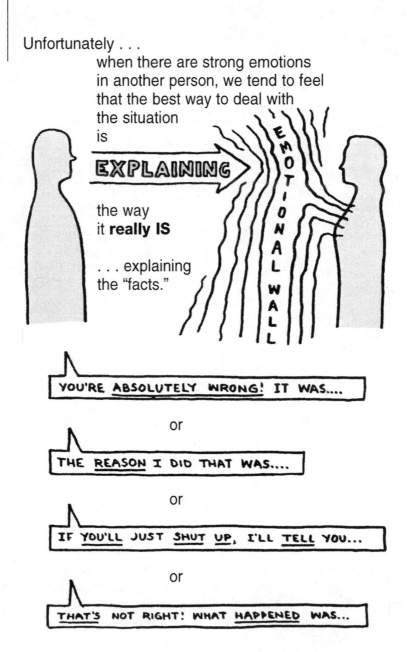

EXPLAINING

EMOTIONAL WALL

the way
it **really IS**

. . . explaining
the "facts."

YOU'RE <u>ABSOLUTELY</u> <u>WRONG!</u> IT WAS....

or

THE <u>REASON</u> I DID THAT WAS....

or

IF <u>YOU'LL</u> JUST <u>SHUT</u> <u>UP</u>, I'LL <u>TELL</u> YOU...

or

<u>THAT'S</u> NOT RIGHT! WHAT <u>HAPPENED</u> WAS...

In reality...
it is the reverse of our natural tendency to "explain" which brings about communication.

It is only **after** we express our **emotional understanding** for the other person . . .

. . . that the other person is
READY TO "HEAR" facts.

"HEARING" comes about in this order:

First — EMOTIONAL UNDERSTANDING
Then — "The facts"

NOT

First — "The facts"
Then — EMOTIONAL UNDERSTANDING

We might imagine emotions as being
**like
steam**
in an
old
fashioned
pressure
cooker

. . . and *"the facts" like the food inside.*

To avoid an explosion, we first reduce the
emotional "pressure." Once the "pressure" of
the emotions has been released it is possible
to take a look at "the facts" with a minimum
amount of trouble.

I'LL SAY IT WOULD!
ALL WE EVER DO IS
SEE YOUR FRIENDS!

YOU'RE TIRED OF
SEEING MY FRIENDS
ALL THE TIME!

WELL, IT'S NOT THAT I
DON'T LIKE THEM, BUT
WE HAVEN'T SEEN GERRY
AND PAT FOR MONTHS!

At this point the
"pressure" has come down to
the level where this person can
express some understanding
of the other's viewpoint, and his
or her own specific needs. Even
so, it is important to continue
confirming that the "deeper
message" of the emotions is
being heard.

YOU MISS THE
RELATIONSHIP
YOU HAD WITH
THEM!

YES, I DO MISS THEM. I LIKE THEM BOTH A LOT!

WELL, TO SEE THEM RIGHT AWAY, WE'D HAVE TO CHANGE OUR PLANS FOR THIS WEEK!

I WOULDN'T WANT TO DO THAT, BUT I WOULD LIKE TO SEE THEM AGAIN SOON.

O.K., I DIDN'T KNOW IT MEANT THAT MUCH TO YOU!

YEAH, IT REALLY DOES I'M GLAD YOU UNDERSTAND HOW I FEEL!

While in this case the reduction of "pressure" was fairly rapid, the time it takes to move from "emotion" to "logic" varies. If the original emotion is very strong, it will take longer.

In clarifying, then, it is important to simply
describe, in our own words, as accurately
as possible, what the other person is feeling.

Generally speaking,
   questions . . .
      comments . . .
         and *"explaining"*

         cause complications,

      and a delay in
      reducing emotional pressure.

> YOU ALWAYS DID THINK I WAS STUPID.

> DIDN'T I TELL YOU HOW SMART YOU
> WERE, JUST LAST WEEK?

This kind of question tends to be of little use.
It simply leads to an argument over "facts,"
where neither person listens, and "yes, but . . ."
is used frequently.

> YOU FEEL THAT I SEE YOU AS STUPID.

is a description of what the other person feels,
and promotes communication.

EVERY TIME I DO SOMETHING NICE FOR YOU, YOU COME BACK WITH SOME NASTY REMARK!

MAYBE I WOULDN'T IF YOU DIDN'T NAG SO MUCH!

This "explanation" and attack is far less helpful than:

YOU FEEL I'M UNAPPRECIATIVE AND CRITICAL.

I SEE WE'RE DOING IT YOUR WAY AGAIN!

WHAT DO YOU MEAN? WE NEVER DO IT MY WAY!

... this again leads to a discussion of "facts" and an escalation of emotions.

BUT

YOU FEEL I'M NOT VERY THOUGHTFUL OF YOU?

... promotes communication.

> YOU'RE ALWAYS TRYING TO TELL ME
> HOW TO RUN MY LIFE!

> THAT'S NOT TRUE!

Comments like this generally create further emotional problems. While clarifying "facts" may be useful at a later time, the above response almost always causes frustration in the other person.

> YOU FEEL I'M BOSSY.

is better.

IN IMPROVING A
RELATIONSHIP
IT IS
NOT

THE
FACTS

that are of
first importance
BUT
HOW EACH PERSON

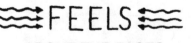

FEELS

ABOUT THE FACTS

Effective listening
means
*demonstrating that we
care enough to hear
the other's viewpoint.*

LOVE

IS

PAYING

ATTENTION

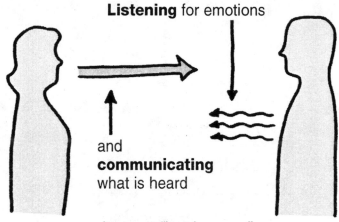

Listening for emotions

and
communicating
what is heard

does not "just happen."
IT REQUIRES

AN ACT OF THE <u>WILL</u>

in which
this person,

after an INTERNAL STRUGGLE

**MAKES
A DECISION**
TO ACT
CREATIVELY.

An act of the will
is needed to
listen *for emotions*
and to
**communicate
*understanding***

especially
when

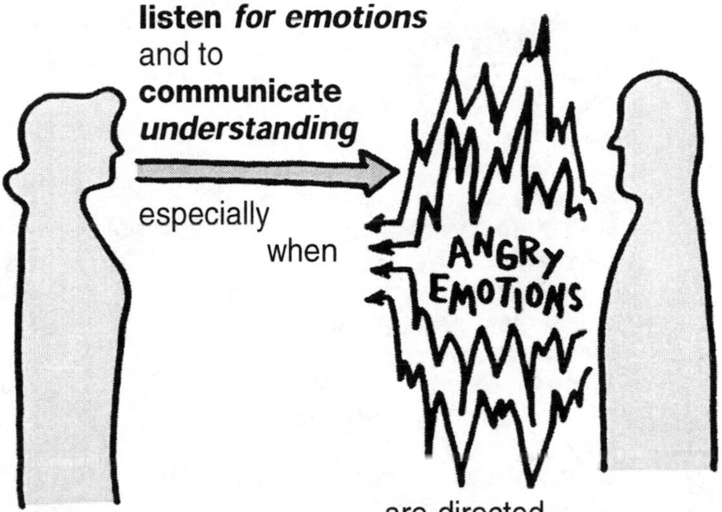

ANGRY
EMOTIONS

are directed
toward us

. . . those **angry emotions**

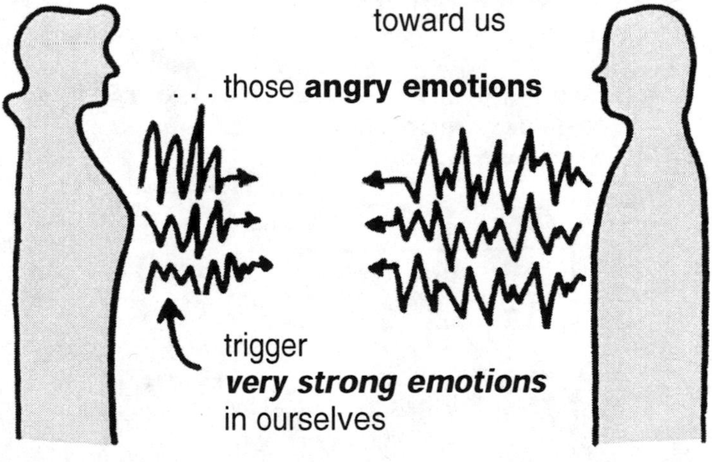

trigger
very strong emotions
in ourselves

We are "reminded" of the childhood situations
when the "big people" were angry with us, ***and
our be-ing was threatened.***

The inner struggle to act creatively might be like this:

ALL RIGHT! IF YOU SAY SO:

UH OH! I CAN FEEL MY ANGER COMING UP.......I'D SURE LIKE TO BLAST HIM BACK........I WONDER HOW MUCH OF THIS ANGER IN ME IS JUSTIFIED BY THIS SITUATION? ......I MIGHT BE USING AN AUTOMATIC WAY OF RELATING TO HIM.......OR HE MIGHT BE RESPONDING IN SOME UNCONSCIOUS WAY TO ME.......... WHO KNOWS?..........IN ANY CASE, HE BELIEVES HE'S FAIR AND RIGHT. ....I CAN'T SEE HOW HE COULD... .....THE "CHILD" IN ME IS PUSHING ME TO TELL HIM OFF ANYWAY.........MY "ADULT" SIDE SAYS LISTEN TO WHAT HE IS SAYING ....HE SOUNDS VERY ANGRY AT ME... ....HE SAYS HE'LL DO IT, BUT HE'S REALLY STEAMING.........WELL, ONE OF US HAS TO DO THE LISTENING FIRST......IT MIGHT AS WELL BE ME........*

YOU SOUND VERY ANGRY WITH ME!

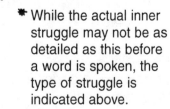

* While the actual inner struggle may not be as detailed as this before a word is spoken, the type of struggle is indicated above.

And other "acts of the will" would be needed to continue acting creatively. It is **most necessary,** but also **most difficult** when we are under attack:

YES, I'M ANGRY.....YOU GIVE ME ALL THE DIRTY JOBS!

HOW CAN HE SAY THAT?.....THAT'S NOT THE WAY I SEE IT....I CAN FEEL MY ANGER COMING UP.... HE REALLY BELIEVES THAT I'M WRONG.....I WANT TO EXPLAIN BUT HE'S NOT READY TO HEAR ME YET.... HE FIRST HAS TO KNOW THAT I UNDERSTAND HOW HE FEELS....

YOU FEEL THAT I'M BEING UNFAIR?...

THAT'S RIGHT! ALL YOU CARE ABOUT IS WHAT'S IN IT FOR YOU

AFTER ALL I'VE DONE FOR HIM!.....WELL, IT'S NOT "THE FACTS" AS I SEE THEM NOW THAT MATTERS BUT UNDERSTANDING HIS FEELINGS.....

I HEAR YOU SAYING THAT I JUST CARE ABOUT MYSELF.

THAT'S RIGHT! I'VE JUST ABOUT HAD IT WITH YOU!

I'M GETTING ANGRY AGAIN MYSELF..... BUT I'D BETTER LISTEN TO HIM

YOU SOUND AS IF YOU'RE REALLY DISGUSTED WITH ME.....

ETC.
ETC.

Generally, it is simpler and clearer if **one person** concentrates on **listening** and **clarifying** (for at least five or ten minutes, but possibly even for an hour, or more in some circumstances).

While this may seem "unfair" for the one listening, it's eventually easier for both. Each person's ability to hear **increases when one or the other focuses on paying attention** while the other talks.

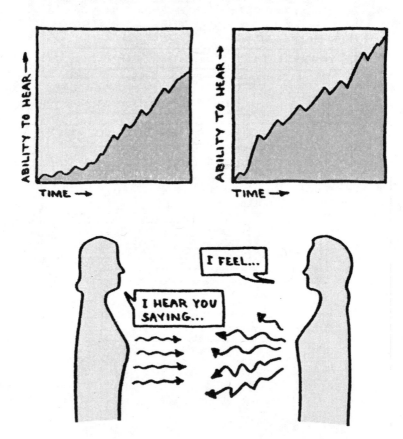

To repeat . . .

Listening for EMOTIONS
and making clear that
we understand
is

MOST DIFFICULT

WHEN WE ARE

UNDER
ATTACK

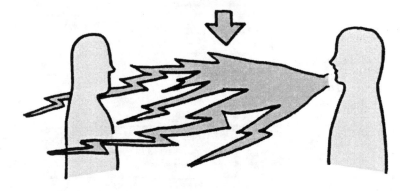

but when this happens,
to **listen with understanding**
without "correcting facts"
is also
MOST NECESSARY.

EXPLAINING "FACTS" WHEN WE ARE ATTACKED PRODUCES A DIALOGUE SUCH AS THIS:

YOU NEVER DID KNOW HOW TO HANDLE MONEY!

WELL, I NEVER SPEND MONEY ON MYSELF LIKE YOU DO!

YEAH? HOW ABOUT THAT NEW OVERCOAT YOU JUST GOT?

THAT WASN'T AN OVERCOAT IT WAS A RAINCOAT — THE FIRST ONE I'VE BOUGHT IN FOUR YEARS.

YOU BOUGHT THAT BLUE JACKET 2½ YEARS AGO.

WHAT ABOUT THE MONEY YOU JUST SPENT ON THAT NEW SUIT?

THAT WAS A SPECIAL OCCASION. YOU KNOW THAT!

I DIDN'T THINK THAT WAS SUCH A SPECIAL OCCASION!

IT CERTAINLY <u>WAS</u>! DON'T YOU REMEMBER...

and it can go on, and on, and on . . .
with increasing frustration.

ON THE OTHER HAND . . .
DESCRIBING THE OTHER'S EMOTIONAL VIEWPOINT
TENDS TO PRODUCE A DIALOGUE
SUCH AS THIS:

> YOU NEVER DID KNOW HOW TO HANDLE MONEY!

> YOU FEEL I'VE SPENT MONEY IN FOOLISH WAYS.

Note that the person describing the other's emotions doesn't just "parrot" back what is said, but tries to **understand** the feeling, and then puts it in **his or her own words**

> "FOOLISH WAYS" IS RIGHT! HOW ABOUT THAT NEW OVERCOAT YOU JUST GOT?

> YOU FEEL THAT WAS A RATHER STUPID WAY TO SPEND MONEY

Note how this statement keeps away from "explanations" and stays with the other's emotional viewpoint

> I'M FED UP WITH THE WAY YOU'RE ALWAYS WASTING MONEY

> YOU SOUND AS IF YOU'VE "HAD IT" WITH ME!

Note again how the topic remains the other's emotional viewpoint.

> YES! WE WOULDN'T BE IN THIS MESS IF IT WEREN'T FOR YOU

> YOU FEEL I'M TO BLAME FOR EVERYTHING!

> I'M NOT SAYING EVERYTHING IS ALL YOUR FAULT...... ......MAYBE I WAS A LITTLE HASTY IN BUYING THAT NEW SUIT......

> YOU FEEL YOU MAY BE PARTLY RESPONSIBLE, TOO

> NOT LIKE YOU ARE..... BUT MAYBE A LITTLE..... ......THE MAIN THING, NOW THOUGH, IS TO FIGURE OUT WHAT TO DO ABOUT THE BIG BILL THAT'S DUE NEXT WEEK!

When what we have said is reflected back to us, we hear what we have said a second time, and begin to reevaluate our words and clarify our thoughts and feelings.

Clarifying does not mean "I agree with your opinion." It does mean *non-judgmental understanding of feelings.*

While communication becomes a problem
when we are attacked, it is also difficult to
clarify what we hear **when the other person
is feeling DEPRESSED.**

Our tendency is to want to **change** the other person
by expressing what seems true to us, rather than
allowing the person to work out their own problem.

Trying to protect a person from sorrow for example,
instead of being helpful may actually make them
feel **more lonely:**

If we can **resist the temptation to "teach"** and
just remain silent - while listening attentively - the
other person will sense our trust in them, and this, in
turn, will help them find strength within themselves.

The following is the type of TRUSTING, LISTENING, and CLARIFYING which promotes movement toward a solution.

Note that the one listening, instead of "giving answers" simply tries to "be with" the other person by putting his or her feelings into words.

The listener's depth of understanding is evident in the fact that instead of mechanically repeating what is said, the emotion is expressed in *the listener's own words.*

YES... THREE PEOPLE IN MY UNIT HAVE ALREADY LEFT.

IT SEEMS IT'S GETTING TOO CLOSE FOR COMFERT!

I WONDER IF I'M NEXT.

YOU FEEL YOU MIGHT LOSE YOUR JOB?

YES! AND THERE'S NOT MUCH AVAILABLE IN MY LINE OF WORK.

I HEAR YOU SAYING YOU DON'T HAVE MUCH HOPE IN FINDING SOMETHING ELSE.

It may seem that the above responses are simply promoting "negative thoughts" instead of offering encouragement and practical advice. Yet, *it is vitally important to continue this type of response until the person in need knows that their emotional viewpoint is understood and accepted.*

Eventually the person speaking will begin to "hear" his or her own words in a deeper way. And, becoming clearer about the situation, they will tentatively and slowly move toward a slightly less negative viewpoint.

Gradually, the person in need will be able to explore possible solutions:

> IS THERE ANY WAY YOU COULD GET TRAINED IN SOMETHING ELSE?

HOWEVER, we are seldom ready to hear about solutions from others until we know we have been heard by them.

It may require a great deal of listening before a person can move from his emotional feelings to the point where various choices can be explored . . .

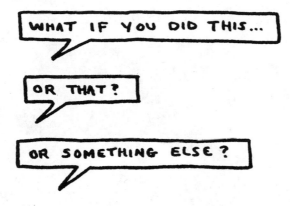

Even when such phrases are used, we need to resist the temptation to say . . .

. . . which tends to make the person feel that he or she is not capable of solving the problem . . . and produces a lack of confidence in his or her own ability when other problems arise.

"CLARIFYING" — demonstrating that we understand — helps another person come into BE-ING.

Just as **watering a plant**

is essential for

be-ing

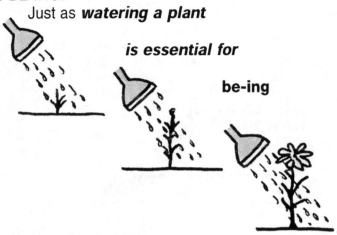

so also,
clarifying that we understand another person's emotions helps that person come into BE-ING.

As children we find it necessary to affirm
that we are of value, over and over again.
When others pay attention to us, it affirms
that we are somebody.

This does not mean that we must constantly pay
attention to children . . . to do so **continually**
would be to give up a part of our **own** BE-ING,
and make us resentful toward the children.
The child soon senses phony love. It's better
to tell the child . . .

I CAN'T WATCH NOW. I'LL SEE IT LATER.

. . . and later give FULL attention.

Full attention for a short time is far better than
1/2 attention for a longer period:

.....UH HUH........UH HUH...........UH HUH......

instead of being helpful, may actually be destructive
in a relationship with children or adults.

When a person **knows** that he or she has been understood, a new atmosphere has been created, and communication not only begins, but **tends to continue . . .**

. . . for just as there is an "emotional inertia" with a *negative* effect . . .

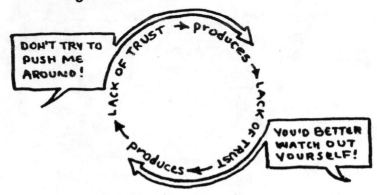

"emotional inertia" can also have a positive effect . . .

TRUST brings back **TRUST** to us.

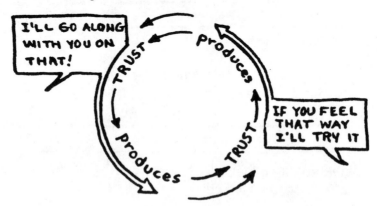

For the sake of the relationship, it may be necessary, temporarily, **not to act on our emotions,** and listen to the other person . . .

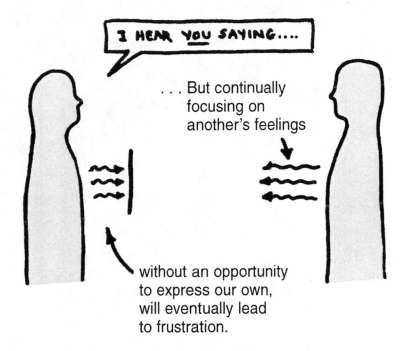

I HEAR YOU SAYING....

. . . But continually focusing on another's feelings

without an opportunity to express our own, will eventually lead to frustration.

Everyone must have a place where his or her own feelings may be expressed to another person and HEARD.

We gain both insight and strength when someone hears us. It is unfortunate that there are so few listeners . . .

because . . .

HEARING
IS
HEALING

SUMMARY

COMMUNICATION comes when, through an inner struggle, we seek to **DEMONSTRATE THAT WE CARE** by:

TRUSTING. Making the conscious effort to "withhold judgment" as to why the other person feels as he or she does.

LISTENING. Trying to discover what the other person is feeling. If uncertain, stating "I don't understand what you're saying."

CLARIFYING. Clarifying that the "deeper message" has been heard by DESCRIBING THE OTHER PERSON'S FEELINGS, as accurately as possible, *without defending ourselves or commenting on what has been said.* Using such words as: **"You** seem to feel. . .," **"You** sound . . . ," "I hear **you** saying . . ."

Note: To "clarify" does **not** mean, "I agree with your opinion." It **does** mean **non-judgmental understanding** of feelings. *Emotions are neither good nor bad, right nor wrong, but simply what we "have" at a particular moment.*

When a person **knows** that we have understood his or her feelings, a new atmosphere is created, and communication begins.

It is important to be aware that the process of
trusting . . . listening . . . and **clarifying**
is not simply a "technique"
but
A MEANS TO A BETTER RELATIONSHIP.
No one likes to feel . . .

But . . .*once we have said something . . .*
we *do* want to know . . .

A useful phrase to communicate **CARING** is

If, in the beginning, the listener keeps responding
with these words with sincerity (not mechanically!)
the relationship will improve for **both.**

Chapter 5

PROTECTING

The other basic step in a relationship is

PROTECTING

. . . FOCUSING ON
 TAKING CARE
 OF OUR
 OWN FEELINGS

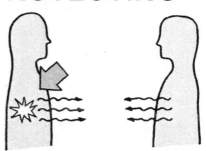

In every close relationship, eventually some point
is reached where there is a disagreement. No matter
how caring or thoughtful each person may be, there
will be a difference of viewpoint about something —
the use of time, the use of money, loyalties, or
something else.

When that happens we may face a struggle within
ourselves about what to do next.

Sometimes "for the sake of the relationship"
we may choose to do what the other person
wants. And this is sometimes the best choice.

Yet, there are also situations where giving up
something we value doesn't "feel right" within us.
And we ask ourselves "How can I keep a good
relationship, and still be true to myself?"

To do this, we need to keep moving back and
forth between REFLECTING and PROTECTING.

Because PROTECTING shifts the focus away from the other person's feelings (at least temporarily), it may create problems in the relationship. So it's vitally important to be clear about what PROTECTING *is*, and how to use it.

PROTECTING IS ABOUT HAVING THE COURAGE TO BE OURSELVES

. . . It's about
having LOVE for our own
"SELF"

Unfortunately many people see

LOVE

as thinking *only* about the person
"out there"

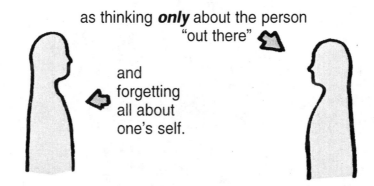

and
forgetting
all about
one's self.

Actually **REAL LOVE** includes

RESPECT for the **"SELF"**
of **ALL** HUMAN BEINGS.

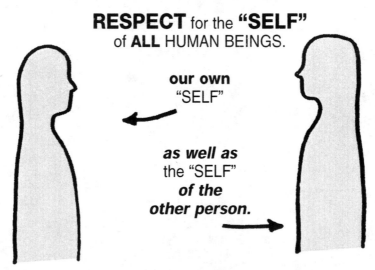

our own
"SELF"

as well as
the "SELF"
*of the
other person.*

"LOVE OTHERS **AS** YOURSELF"

If we think of love as "giving in to the needs of others" we may actually be more irritating to others than helpful to them . . .

To simply say

is so much easier for both!

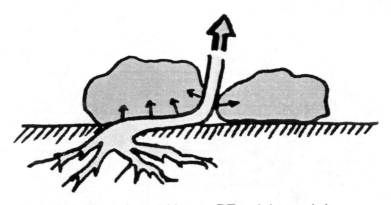

Just as a plant, in seeking to BE, might push its way through some rocks — not allowing the surroundings to keep it from existing — so also, as humans, we have a need to protect ourselves from **"not be-ing."**

"The courage to be is the ethical act in which a [person] affirms his own being in spite of [the] elements of his existence which conflict with his essential self-affirmation."

— Paul Tillich

Physically, we all occupy a certain area of the earth, which for that moment, is "our own."

This "territory" which we consider "ours" . . .

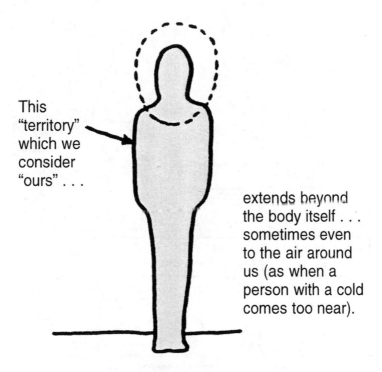

extends beyond the body itself . . . sometimes even to the air around us (as when a person with a cold comes too near).

Our "be-ing" depends on protecting that territory. It is not selfish in a negative sense to simply want to "be." Such "be-ing" is a part of life — in fact, it is life.

Imagine sitting with a friend . . .
when another
friend phones
you

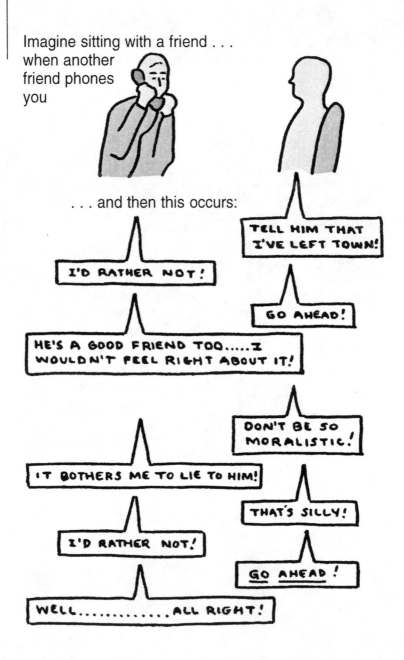

. . . and then this occurs:

In such a situation, the other person has invaded our "emotional territory" and we have given

away

a part

of our

"SELF"

Even though we have allowed it to happen,
resentment will follow
within ourselves, and toward the other person,
because there has been a lack of "SELF" respect
for both ourselves and the other person.

We are actually surrounded by many kinds of territories which affect our be-ing in a variety of ways

If another person **forces himself** into our territory, **even with our permission,** we can expect to feel both anger toward ourselves (for allowing it to happen), and resentment toward the other person (for not respecting our "SELF")

MISUNDERSTANDINGS come about because we **ASSUME** that the other person *should know* the limits of

. . . *but what may be an "infringement of territory" for one person* (as in the previous example of the phone call), *may hardly affect another person in the same situation:*

Because "territories" are not always clearly evident, we have a responsibility to

DEFINE
THAT AREA
WHICH IS OUR

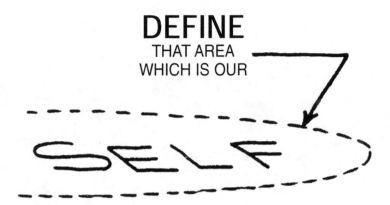

"territorial limits",
both physical, and emotional,
are **defined** by

THE "OUCH!" LINE

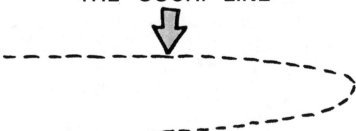

Our "territory" is that area **within which** another person is causing us **continuous** pain — that area within which our be-ing is affected.

The location of the "ouch!" line
is determined by the person
WITHIN the territory, rather than by
the person outside of it

. . . for while
another
person
might
guess
the limits
of another's
territory . . .

only the person within it knows the exact point
where pain is felt.

For example . . .

To step on another person's foot
may or may not be painful.
*Only the person whose
territory is being affected
knows the
precise location
on the
"ouch" line . . .*

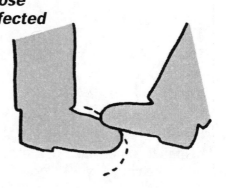

While most of us would have little problem telling another person about something that affects us physically — such as: "You're stepping on my toe!" — we may tend to feel that protecting emotional territory is "not being loving" — that it is "selfish" and uncaring.

YET . . .

To "suffer silently" is not fair either to ourselves, *or the other person,* for it creates "underground" problems in the relationship, which the other person often finds difficult to understand:

Instead of "suffering silently" it is usually far more helpful to simply **DEFINE** that which is "ours." ("It hurts me when you do that.")

DEFINING emotional "ouch!" lines would be seen in statements such as these in which we make our emotion known:

> I'M FINDING IT DIFFICULT TO READ WITH THAT MUSIC SO LOUD. WOULD YOU PLEASE TURN IT DOWN A LITTLE.

and

> I'D RATHER NOT SPEND THE EVENING WITH HIM. WOULD YOU ASK SOMEONE ELSE?

and

> I'M SORRY, I NEVER LEND THAT TO ANYONE. IT WAS A GIFT FROM A VERY SPECIAL PERSON!

and

> I CAN'T TALK ANY LONGER WITH YOU NOW. I HAVE SOME THINGS TO DO.

It is ultimately better to let another person know when he or she is over the "ouch!" line (It may not be clear!) than to continually relate on a basis of false "politeness."

DEFINING OUR TERRITORY then, simply means
DESCRIBING THAT WHICH IS OUR OWN
("My feelings are . . . ")

WITHOUT

TRYING TO

CHANGE THE

OTHER PERSON.

Problems are seldom
solved by words
such as:

For most people such a phrase triggers off
childhood emotions of inferiority . . .

. . . and the need to be in power:

and the need to "put down" to regain power:

. . . and the process is again reversed.
Such struggles generally continue with little
or no progress, benefiting neither person, and
leaving both exhausted and emotionally drained.

On the other hand, if instead of giving
"ADVICE"

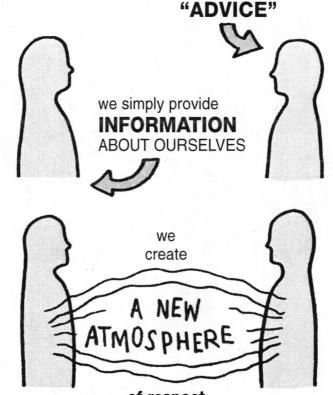

we simply provide
INFORMATION
ABOUT OURSELVES

we
create

A NEW
ATMOSPHERE

of respect
in the relationship
because

"ADVICE" says "YOU ARE A **CHILD"**
("You aren't capable of leading your own life")
while
"INFORMATION" says "YOU ARE AN **ADULT"**
("I respect your right to choose what you do based
on the information I give you")

While hearing **ADVICE**

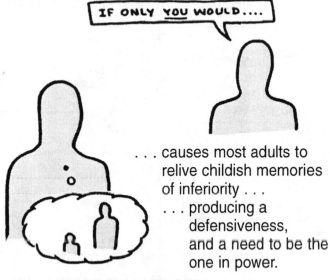

IF ONLY <u>YOU</u> WOULD....

. . . causes most adults to
relive childish memories
of inferiority . . .
. . . producing a
defensiveness,
and a need to be the
one in power.

When only **INFORMATION** is given

THE WAY I
SEE IT IS......

. . . we hear *respect* from
the other, and, because
the other *isn't trying
to change us there
is no need to "be the
one in power."*

Examples of **ADVICE** are:	Examples of **INFORMATION** are:
WHEN ARE YOU GOING TO STOP BEING SO IRRITATING?	I GET IRRITATED WHEN YOU DO THAT.
DON'T YOU REALIZE IT'S TIME TO EAT?	I'D LIKE TO EAT SOON.
DO YOU CALL THAT MAKING LOVE?	I LIKED IT WHEN.......
I THINK YOU'D BETTER WEAR YOUR COAT!	IT'S VERY COLD TODAY
DON'T DRIVE SO FAST!	DRIVING THIS FAST BOTHERS ME!

However, A WORD OF CAUTION: it is not easy to simply "provide information."

This is especially difficult for very intelligent people who see "clear reasoning" as the primary way to improve a relationship.

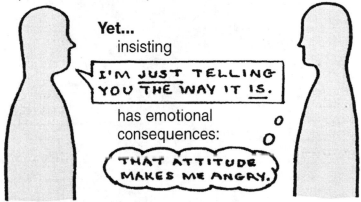

Effectiveness in giving information is not simply found in the words that are used, but much more in the speaker's attitude of openness to hear another's viewpoint.

Listeners usually clearly sense the difference between neutral information and a forceful attempt to change them. Often, the response to an arrogant attitude is to silently withdraw from the relationship.

Unfortunately, problems are often created when we care deeply about being the person who is "right". If so, it may be wise to delay our reacton overnight. (Maybe even longer!).

But now back to the telephone situation mentioned previously. Here's an example of defining territory in a healthy way:

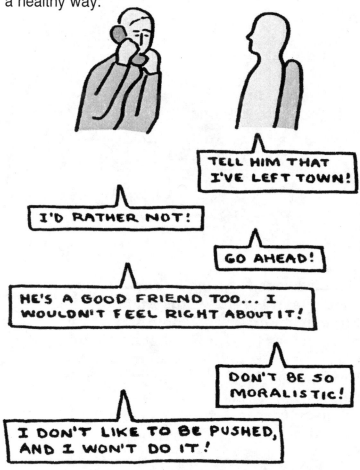

NOTE, that in this comment, the person is simply *stating his own position,* but not attacking the other person with a cutting remark (such as "At least I'm not a hypocrite like *you* are!").

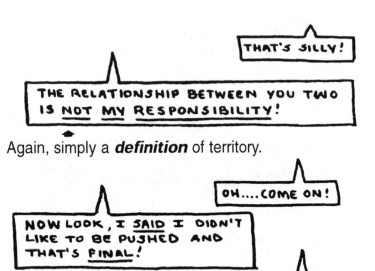

Again, simply a **definition** of territory.

Defending, but
not attacking.

While responses such as these
may temporarily strain the relationship, the
honesty of the response generally promotes
mutual respect.

**In fact, such directness may later
even deepen a relationship:**

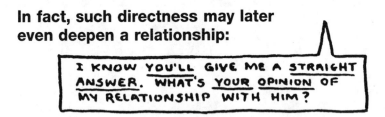

When one person is quietly "giving in" there is
no REAL relationship anyway, only a superficial
one.

But sometimes, even after we define our feelings,
the response may be:

I DON'T CARE IF IT DOES HURT YOU!

We then face the practical question:

SUPPOSE

WE

DEFINE

OUR

"OUCH!" LINE

AND

IT'S

NOT RESPECTED?

We then **DEFEND** ourselves

by

Quietly stating what we will do
under various circumstances:

> IF YOU DO THAT, THEN
> I'LL.....
> AND IF YOU DO THE
> OTHER, THEN I'LL.....

This is **NOT A THREAT . . .**

> IF YOU DON'T SHAPE UP, I'LL.....

NOR WHINING . . .

> WHY CAN'T YOU HELP ME?......

BUT INFORMATION about ourselves:

> I'M SORRY, BUT I HAVE TO DO THIS
> FOR MY OWN SELF RESPECT.

An example of "defending":

Note that this is *not a threat* — "If you ***don't*** I'll get someone who ***will!***" — but rather a quiet expression of SELF RESPECT

DEFENDING
ourselves

also means

TAKING
APPROPRIATE
ACTION

. . . demonstrating responsibility
by acting on what we said we would do.

> I HIRED SOMEONE TODAY
> TO MAKE THOSE REPAIRS.

> ARE YOU OUT OF YOUR MIND?
> I TOLD YOU A COUPLE OF WEEKS
> AGO THAT I WOULD DO IT.!!

> I KNOW YOU WANT TO FIX
> IT, BUT I RESPECT MYSELF
> TOO MUCH TO USE IT ANY
> LONGER WHEN IT'S BROKEN.

This is not an attack,
but simply "protection
of territory."

Sometimes our territory may have become so small, by consistently "giving in," that there is little left.

When we have allowed this to happen, we may find that we are "taken for granted," and may eventually become resentful.

Usually it is easier for ourselves and others if territory that has been given up is regained *gradually.*

It is helpful to start reclaiming our territory in a
relatively small area.

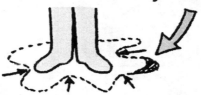

Such an approach slowly builds confidence in our own self worth. Reclaiming territory *will* anger others who "don't expect that" from us. (But we must be prepared to face such anger; after all, we did allow it to happen!) . . .however, doing it *gradually* gives time for everyone (including ourselves) to adjust to the new situation.

Regaining our *selves* comes about through phrases such as these:

> IT'S SOMEONE ELSES TURN TO CLEAN UP.

> I WOULD MIND DOING THAT.

> I'VE DECIDED THAT IF YOU FORGET IT AGAIN, YOU'LL HAVE TO GET IT YOURSELF.

In summary, then

HAVING THE COURAGE TO BE

means

DEFINING and, if necessary,

DEFENDING our territory,

NOT TELLING THE OTHER
WHAT THEY SHOULD DO:

BUT

1. MAKING OUR EMOTIONS KNOWN

2. QUIETLY INFORMING
THE OTHER, if necessary,
OF OUR
PLAN OF ACTION

3. TAKING NEEDED
APPROPRIATE ACTION

Paradoxically . . .

LOVING OURSELVES

FREES US TO LOVE OTHERS
AND
MAKES IT EASIER FOR OTHERS
TO LOVE US

When we do *not* take responsibility for our own self (by defining and defending our territory) we feel a "lack of love" and may turn to manipulating others to get the love we "deserve."

On the other hand, when we take responsibility for our own needs then the other person no longer feels obligated to help, and can experience real joy in giving. Freedom to give makes love possible.

Loving ourselves frees us to love others — and makes it easier for others to love us.

SOLVING PROBLEMS

Chapter 6

EXPLORING ALTERNATIVES

We also act creatively
in a "power" situation
when we

EXPLORE

ALTERNATIVES

WITH

SELF

RESPECT

"EXPLORING ALTERNATIVES WITH SELF RESPECT"

MEANS
SORTING THROUGH
VARIOUS SOLUTIONS
TRYING TO
DISCOVER

THAT SOLUTION WHICH DOES NOT INFRINGE ON EITHER PERSONS SELF

Most struggles center around

"A PROBLEM"

and the

MEANING

that the solution has for each person.

For example . . .

IF

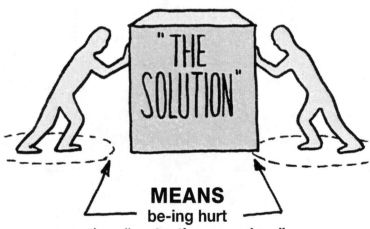

MEANS
be-ing hurt
then **"protecting ourselves"**
will claim all our attention and
we are not free to look elsewhere —
to explore alternatives with self respect.

In exploring how our *framework* of MEANING affects relationships, consider how our *viewpoint* determines what is seen in this illustration.

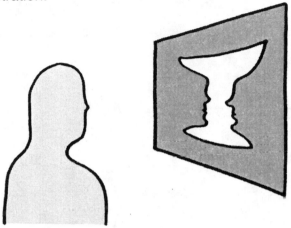

If it is seen as a "vase" then the details of the outline have a certain meaning, (the contours of the vase) . . .

. . . but if the **meaning** we bring to the picture is "two faces in profile" then the details of those same lines are seen quite differently.

The **meaning** we bring to every situation has an effect on **how we see:**

If three people are looking at an open field . . .

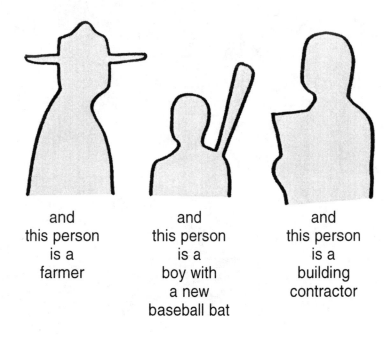

| and this person is a farmer | and this person is a boy with a new baseball bat | and this person is a building contractor |

. . . each will see that same field in a somewhat different way. The framework of MEANING determines the details.

The over-all meaning we give to a relationship determines our actions.

If the relationship MEANS

PROTECTING OURSELVES

our words and actions
will "fit in" with that meaning:

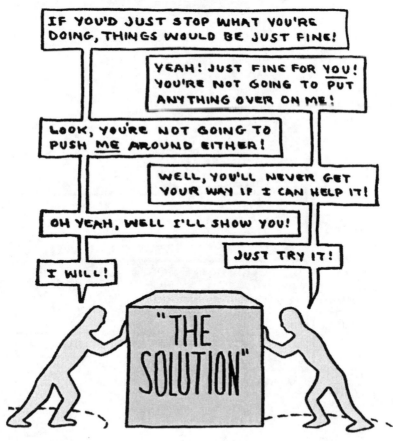

On the other hand,
if the relationship
MEANS

EXPLORING ALTERNATIVES
WITH SELF RESPECT

then our words and actions will "fit in"
with *that* meaning, and the problem solutions
can be set aside.

Our minds work in such a way that *we cannot bring* **TWO MEANINGS** *to something* **AT THE SAME TIME.**

Either we see **"the vase"** or **"the faces"** **— but not both at the same moment.**

In this illustration it is a relatively simple matter to change the over-all viewpoint and give an entirely different meaning to the details.

In human relationships, however, to change the over-all viewpoint is far more difficult.

Because we cannot give TWO MEANINGS
to something at the same time, when
strong emotions are present, it's
almost impossible to change the
focus of meaning
from
"EMOTION" to "LOGIC"
because
we must choose
either one, **or** the other,
and emotions have
a stronger claim on our attention.

Yet when **EITHER** person

DEMONSTRATES CARING
by choosing the priority of
emotional understanding
over arguing, by

TRUSTING

LISTENING and

CLARIFYING

then it becomes easier *to change the focus of
attention to another "framework of meaning."*

BUT usually
alternative solutions ("FACTS")
can only be explored
AFTER
the other person feels
HEARD AND UNDERSTOOD.

We keep moving toward a solution when we *focus on exploring alternatives* with "self" respect, and *keep information moving back and forth* between us.

THE BANK WON'T LEND US
ANY MORE RIGHT NOW.

Sometimes when information is being exchanged
*emotional problems arise which cloud the free
exchange of information.*

IF YOU HADN'T WASTED MONEY
ON THAT OTHER EQUIPMENT,
WE WOULDN'T BE IN THIS MESS!

At such a point it is necessary to return
(perhaps again and again), to focusing
on the emotions . . . trusting . . . listening . . .
clarifying . . . before continuing with the "facts."

YOU FEEL THAT WAS
A FOOLISH EXPENSE.

Once the emotions have been, "heard,"
it will be possible to return again to the "facts" . . .

The following questions will help maintain a focus, while moving toward a solution.

Answers to some of the questions will be quite obvious, others may require considerable thought. It depends on the specific problem.

Rather than work through each question in detail, it will be useful to use the questions as
A PROBLEM SOLVING CHECK LIST*

1. **What** specifically is to be solved?

2. **When** must it be solved?

3. Is it possible to **expand the time available** before a final decision must be made?

4. What are the **limits** within which we must work — those things that probably won't change? (Could any of these limits be changed, though costly?)

5. Has the main **meaning** of the problem for **each person** been made clear?

6. Has holding on to a **particular solution** become more important than what needs to be done?

8. Am I remaining open to a **new and unfamiliar solution** to the problem?

9. What is the **next step**?

10. Am I checking **within myself,** emotionally and spiritually, to see if this choice "feels right"?

*For **comments on this check list** see page **235**

SUMMARY OF STEPS TO BE TAKEN IN MOVING FROM A POWER STRUGGLE TO A CREATIVE RELATIONSHIP

It is important to be aware that each step does not automatically lead to the next. In the process of moving toward a creative relationship, it may be necessary to return and repeat previous steps before continuing.

1. *Realizing* that all emotions are acceptable (but not all actions).

2. *Trusting* — Making a conscious effort to withhold judgment (not "pushing" our own viewpoint).

3. *Listening* — Trying to hear the other's emotional viewpoint.

4. *Clarifying* — Demonstrating our willingness to listen by making clear what feelings have been heard before discussing the "facts."

5. *Defining* — Clarifying our own territory, by making emotions known.

6. *Defending* — Protecting our territory, by quietly stating choices and taking action when needed.

7. *Exploring Alternatives* — Examining other solutions with self respect.

Risking - Being willing to face change
In contrast to most of the steps above, which generally move from one to the other in the order listed, "risking" is a part of the process and is usually helpful at any point.

Chapter 7

RISKING AWARENESS

While the ideal situation is one in which **both persons are willing to explore alternatives with self respect,** often the relationship is such that this cannot happen . . .

WHAT THEN,

CAN WE DO

WHEN THE

OTHER PERSON

WILL NOT

COOPERATE?

In such a situation,
we may also have to

RISK

A CHANGE

IN OUR

OWN

POSITION

Often we are kept from acting creatively because *we feel comfortable with that which is familiar.*

Understandably,

all of us find that

the **FAMILIAR** means

<u>SECURITY</u>

and that which is

STRANGE or DIFFERENT

means

INSECURITY

Yet,

GROWTH

INVOLVES

<u>RISK</u>

"An essential aspect of creativity
is not being afraid to fail."
—Edwin Land

1. Often the reason the other person will not cooperate is that we are not willing to **RISK seeing OURSELVES as we are.**

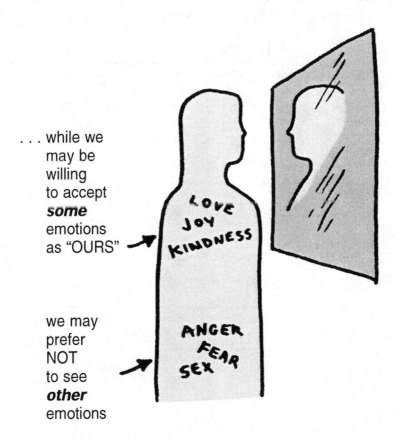

. . . while we may be willing to accept **some** emotions as "OURS" →

LOVE JOY KINDNESS

we may prefer NOT to see **other** emotions →

ANGER FEAR SEX

. . . because it seems that having those emotions means that we are "bad" or "unacceptable."

When we try to hide our emotions from ourselves, others see our defensiveness and are less trustful of the relationship . . .

Typical defensive remarks:

ME AFRAID? HEH...HEH...THAT DOESN'T BOTHER ME ONE SINGLE BIT!

I'M GLAD I HAVE A PURE MIND AS FAR AS SEX IS CONCERNED!

I CAN'T UNDERSTAND WHY PEOPLE GET ANGRY. I LOVE EVERYBODY!

Sometimes it is possible to deny our feelings so continually that we not longer have **conscious** awareness of certain emotions.

However, when we accept ourselves as we are, our relationships with others change because we have an "openness" that puts others at ease.

Typical "open" remarks:

> I GUESS I REALLY AM THAT WAY, AND I'D BETTER FACE IT!

> I SEE NOW THAT I REALLY DIDN'T MEAN THAT. I JUST SAID IT SO SHE'D LIKE ME.

> THIS SITUATION IS REALLY GETTING ME UP TIGHT. I CAN FEEL IT IN MY STOMACH!

and sometimes we may hear the reply:

> YOU KNOW....I FEEL THE SAME WAY!

2. Another reason the other person may not cooperate, is that we may not be willing to **RISK** the **other person's seeing us as we are.**

If we set up a phony
image of ourselves to
relate to, the other
person cannot know
who we really "are"

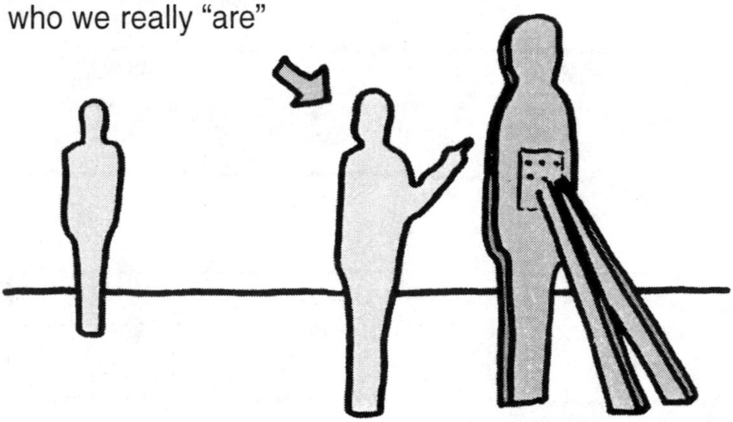

. . . and we actually communicate "I want your cooperation, but I don't trust you enough to let you know who I am."

We hide ourselves behind remarks such as . . .

A real relationship only becomes possible when we are willing to reveal our emotions to another.

Unfortunately,
rather than risk rejection
we may settle for a
relationship
that
is

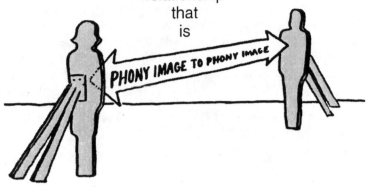

. . . when it is possible to have a
creative relationship
that
is

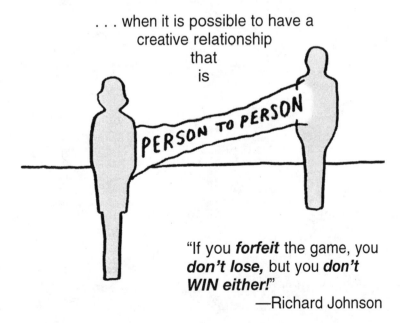

"If you ***forfeit*** the game, you
don't lose, but you ***don't
WIN either!***"
—Richard Johnson

3. Sometimes when the *other person* will *not cooperate* it may be necessary to **RISK** a **change in the relationship itself**.

In understanding what this means it might be helpful to visualize a relationship as like being on a see-saw with another person:

When we see that the relationship is "out-of-balance" our tendency is to point a finger at the other person and tell him or her . . .

IF YOU WOULD JUST MOVE CLOSER TO ME WE'D BE BACK IN BALANCE!

THIS person often does not realize that the *"pressure"* to get the other person to change their position is *actually keeping the other person away*.

"PRESSURE" on the other person in an attempt to "get love" is seen in phrases like these . . .

YOU NEVER PAY ANY ATTENTION TO WHAT I DO!

DON'T MY TEARS MEAN ANYTHING TO YOU?

YOU'RE MY WHOLE LIFE! WITHOUT YOU IT'S NOTHING!

WHY CAN'T YOU SHOW SOME APPRECIATION FOR MY WORK?

WHY CAN'T YOU BE MORE AFFECTIONATE?

YOU NEVER SPEND ANY TIME WITH ME!

A change in the "balance" of the relationship may
also occur
if
this
person . . .

**_feels good enough
about herself or himself
to risk "not being close"_**

                    and
            backs away.

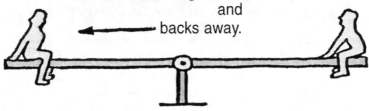

Typical "risking" statements:

> I HAVE TOO MUCH SELF RESPECT TO
> KEEP TAKING THAT ANYMORE.

> I'M <u>VERY</u> ANGRY WITH YOU.

> I'VE DECIDED THAT IT'S BEST
> TO BE APART FOR A WHILE.

and . . .

> **I'M FED UP WITH YOUR PUSHING ME AROUND.**

> **IT'S TOO PAINFUL FOR ME TO CONTINUE THIS RELATIONSHIP.**

. . . all are phrases of
self respect.

Such "risking the relationship" has a "freeing" effect on the other person, because he or she no longer has to ask, *"How can I deal with this pressure?"* but is free to ask: *"What do we want in this relationship?"*

OFTEN when pressure has been removed, the person who has been pressured will, on his or her own accord, move closer again.

To "RISK THE RELATIONSHIP ITSELF"
means an *actual risk* rather than a "bluff" or a
"threat" to manipulate the other person.

A "bluff" or a "threat" is destructive rather
than helpful, because manipulation of another
means a lack of respect and love.

It neither provides

**"Conditions that make it easy for
the other person to BE somebody."**

. . . nor does it include

"The courage to BE ourselves."

Although "risking" may sometimes create other
problems in a relationship, it is usually better than
continuously suffering in silence, and never
knowing the possibilities of creative solutions.

We learn and grow through choices.

Some relationships, however,
may reach the point where,
if they continue, one or the other's
"self" will continually be hurt.

To risk a relationship
may mean that the
best solution is to
leave the relationship
and go elsewhere.

A complete break
in a relationship is
usually not necessary,
however. Standing up
for one's self may simply
mean a break in the "old"
type of relationship,
and accepting a
"new" relationship
with the same person
("a re-negotiation
of the 'contract'").

A couple of thoughts:
"If you don't ask the answer is no."
and
"It's easier to criticize than be correct."

While we must face the fact that

NOT ALL PROBLEMS
CAN BE
"SOLVED"

no matter what the conditions are,
it is always possible to

IMPROVE THE SITUATION

when
we are willing
for others,
and ourselves,
to

"BE"

SUMMARY EXAMPLES

1. IN A HOME
2. AT WORK

SUMMARY EXAMPLE #1: **IN A HOME**

> WELL, I SEE YOU'VE MADE A MESS OF THINGS, AS USUAL!

1. *Realizing all emotions are acceptable,*
(but not all actions).

> OH...HE'S REALLY BUGGING ME TODAY!
> THAT CONSTANT CRITICISM IS TOO MUCH!
> ...I HATE HIM FOR THAT!....WHAT'S THE
> MATTER WITH ME?....I MUST BE AN AWFUL
> PERSON TO HAVE THAT ANGER....NO, THAT'S
> NOT TRUE. ANY FEELING I HAVE IS O.K.! IT'S
> THERE FOR A PURPOSE...BUT I DON'T HAVE
> TO ACT ON IT...

2. *Trusting — Making a conscious effort to
withhold judgment* (not "pushing"
our own viewpoint).

> I'D STILL LIKE TO TELL HIM OFF, THOUGH!
> IT'S INCREDIBLE HOW I ALWAYS GET THE
> BLAME...I CAN'T UNDERSTAND HIS
> ATTITUDE!....WELL, KNOWING HOW HIS
> MOTHER PUSHED HIM AROUND, MAYBE I
> CAN UNDERSTAND PART OF IT....I'M
> STILL TEMPTED TO "PUSH" BACK, BUT
> THAT WON'T HELP EITHER OF US....
> I'D BETTER LISTEN....

> I DON'T UNDERSTAND WHAT YOU MEAN....

> NATURALLY! YOU'RE SO STUPID, YOU NEVER UNDERSTAND ANYTHING! ...YOU DIDN'T SEND THE MONEY FOR THE VACATION COTTAGE, LIKE I TOLD YOU TO DO! GET IT?!!

3. Listening — *Trying to hear the other's emotional viewpoint.*

> WHEEEW! I HEAR HIM LOUD AND CLEAR! HE'S FURIOUS ABOUT MY NOT SENDING THAT MONEY!

4. Clarifying — *Demonstrating our willingness to hear by making clear what feelings have been heard before discussing "facts."*

> EXPLAINING WON'T HELP NOW! FIRST HE'S GOT TO KNOW THAT I CARE ENOUGH ABOUT OUR RELATIONSHIP TO HEAR WHAT HE IS SAYING...."DESCRIBE HIS FEELINGS IN MY OWN WORDS."....HE'S MADE ME SO ANGRY IT'S NOT EASY....BUT HERE GOES....

A slight
softening
of the anger

At this point
the emotional pressure is not as strong
as it was, but confirmation of willingness
to hear must continue *until the person
attacking knows that their emotional
viewpoint has been heard.*

YOU FEEL I'M LIVING IN MY OWN LITTLE DREAM WORLD, AND NOT VERY AWARE OF WHAT'S GOING ON WITH YOU!

A reflection of his feeling - not an agreement!

THAT'S JUST THE WAY I FEEL!

The ideal response!

The process of trusting, listening and clarifying must continue until emotional pressure has been reduced to the point where clarification of territory can be discussed.

I'VE LISTENED TO YOU, NOW I'D LIKE TO TELL YOU HOW I FEEL.

GO AHEAD!

5. Defining — Clarifying our own territory by making our emotions known.

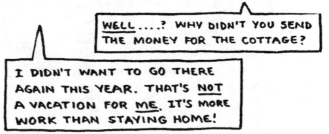

WELL....? WHY DIDN'T YOU SEND THE MONEY FOR THE COTTAGE?

I DIDN'T WANT TO GO THERE AGAIN THIS YEAR. THAT'S NOT A VACATION FOR ME. IT'S MORE WORK THAN STAYING HOME!

Defining territory often leads to a further attack and, if it is intense, previous steps in listening may again have to be repeated.

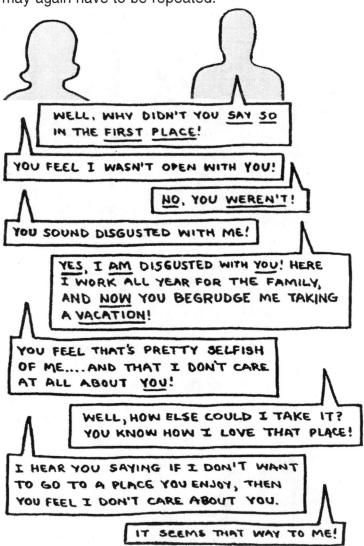

> I KNOW YOU WORK HARD, AND I WANT YOU TO
> ENJOY YOUR VACATION. I JUST DON'T WANT
> TO SPEND THAT TIME WORKING.

Again, territory has been defined. Even so, the other person may not agree. To "give in" at this point "for the sake of the relationship" is a superficial solution. We will have resentment, both within ourselves, and for the other person, when a person remains over our "ouch!" line.

6. *Defending — Protecting our territory by quietly stating choices and taking appropriate action.*

> IF YOU INSIST ON GOING, SOMEONE ELSE
> WILL HAVE TO DO THE COOKING AND CLEANING.

> I DON'T SEE WHY YOU SAY THAT.
> YOU USUALLY DO THAT AT HOME.

> WITH THAT AND MY JOB, I NEED A
> VACATION AS MUCH AS YOU DO!

> WELL..........YEAH..........I
> SUPPOSE YOU DO

> IF WE DECIDE TO GO THERE, YOU SHOULD
> UNDERSTAND THAT I DON'T WANT TO
> WORK....BUT IF WE DECIDE NOT TO GO, I'M
> WILLING TO LOOK INTO OTHER POSSIBILITIES.

Before the problem is resolved, still other situations may arise which necessitate listening on the part of the other person before going further — reversing the previous roles of speaker and listener.

For example, the couple might go to bed before the problem has been solved:

DON'T TOUCH ME! HOW DO YOU EXPECT ME TO MAKE LOVE AFTER THE WAY YOU TREATED ME TODAY?

YOU FEEL THAT I WAS UNFAIR THIS AFTERNOON, AND YOU'RE STILL VERY ANGRY ABOUT IT.

AFTER WHAT HAPPENED, YOU CAN'T EXPECT ME TO JUST FLIP A SWITCH AND TURN ON THE AFFECTION!

YOU'RE SAYING THAT YOU CAN'T CHANGE YOUR EMOTIONS THAT QUICKLY.

I FEEL YOU'RE JUST USING ME.

YOU CAN'T UNDERSTAND HOW I COULD REALLY CARE ABOUT YOU AFTER THE THINGS I SAID...AND YOU FEEL USED.

IT'S HARD TO BELIEVE THAT YOU LOVE ME AFTER THE WAY YOU PUT ME DOWN!

It's tempting for the listener to want to "comment" or "explain" here, but the person is not ready to hear. Further confirmation of feelings are needed first.

IT MAKES YOU QUESTION MY SINCERITY....

WELL...HOW ELSE COULD I FEEL? IT'S PRETTY OBVIOUS ISN'T IT?

YOU FEEL IT'S OBVIOUS THAT I DON'T LOVE YOU AT ALL.

WELL, I KNOW YOU CARE SOMETIMES, BUT YOU HURT ME VERY DEEPLY TODAY.

The anger softens a little here

IT WAS PAINFUL FOR YOU... HUH?

YES...

The intensity of the emotion here is so great that it will not be resolved without a great deal more listening . . . Even in this brief exchange, however, the beginning of a change of mood can be seen.

207

7. Exploring Alternatives — Examining other solutions with self respect.

And the next day when discussion resumes . . .

> I DON'T FEEL ANY DIFFERENTLY TODAY ABOUT WHAT I SAID YESTERDAY. I STILL DON'T WANT TO SPEND VACATION TIME WORKING IN THE COTTAGE.

> I'VE BEEN THINKING ABOUT IT, AND I CAN UNDERSTAND HOW YOU WOULD FEEL THAT WAY. BUT HOW WAS I TO KNOW THAT IT BOTHERED YOU....YOU NEVER SAID ANYTHING ABOUT IT BEFORE THIS.

> IT'S BOTHERED ME FOR YEARS. I GUESS I SHOULD HAVE TOLD YOU LONG BEFORE THIS.

Yes! Defining the "ouch!" line is the responsibility of the person *within it.*

> I WONDER IF WE COULD WORK OUT SOMETHING THAT WOULD BE O.K. WITH US BOTH.

> LIKE WHAT?

> **WELL, HOW ABOUT EATING ALL OUR MEALS IN THAT RESTAURANT IN TOWN?**

> **THAT'S SO EXPENSIVE I COULDN'T ENJOY IT AND NEITHER WOULD YOU!**

◄ It's helpful for her to define her "ouch!" line.
◄ Unfortunately she goes on and defines **his** too.

When we define another's territory the person may become irritated and not know quite why. Actually it brings back the childhood feeling of "You have to be told for your own good." It is subtly giving "advice" rather than "information."

He's somewhat bothered, but still open to "exploring alternatives." ►

> **IF I DIDN'T WANT TO DO IT I WOULDN'T HAVE SUGGESTED IT ......DO YOU HAVE A BETTER IDEA?**

> **HOW ABOUT GOING TO TURTLEBACK LODGE?**

A definition of ► his territory

> **NO....I WANT TO GO TO A PLACE WHERE I CAN FISH.**

Using the problem check list (page 179) might be useful at this point.

A Problem Check List (See pages 235 to 250)

1. What, specifically, is to be solved?

We both want an enjoyable and restful vacation.

2. When must it be solved?

Within the month.

3. Is it possible to **expand the time available** before a final decision is made?

Not necessary.

4. What are the **limits** within which we must work? (Could any of these limits be changed, though costly?)

Little or no housework.
Fishing available.
Can't spend more than $1200.

5. Has the main **meaning** of the problem **for each person been made clear?**

Yes.

6. Has holding on to a *particular solution* become more important than what needs to be done?

No.

7. What *resources* are available to solve the problem?

Friends

Travel Agency

8. Is there openness to a *new and unfamiliar solution* to the problem?

A vacation with some housework and without fishing would be considered if it is enjoyable and restful for both.

9. What is the *next step?*

Check with friends and travel agency to explore other possibilities.

10.. Am I checking *within myself,* emotionally and spiritually, to see if this choice "feels right"?

So far o.k. - to be rechecked later.

WELL, WHAT DID YOU FIND OUT ABOUT THE VACATION POSSIBILITIES?

I ASKED A LOT OF PEOPLE BUT NOTHING SOUNDED VERY GOOD TO ME..... WHAT ABOUT YOU?

MOST OF THE FRIENDS I TALKED WITH GO TO THE SAME PLACE EACH YEAR JUST AS WE DO................ AND THEN I GOT TO THINKING......... WHY DON'T WE DO SOMETHING ENTIRELY DIFFERENT THIS YEAR?

FOR INSTANCE?

Risking — Being willing to face change.

..........WELL........I'VE BEEN THINKING ABOUT THE JOHNSONS. THEY APPRECIATED BEING OUR GUESTS AT THE COTTAGE BEFORE THEY MOVED.......AND THEY'VE BEEN BEGGING US TO VISIT THEM IN THEIR NEW HOME.........

YEAH?....?

.........I'M AFRAID YOU'RE GOING TO LAUGH AT ME, OR BE ANGRY.........BUT..... WELL.. ...I CHECKED INTO IT.....AND WE COULD FLY THERE AND BACK FOR $500.......AND WE HAVEN'T SEEN THEM FOR A WHILE.....

WELL, IT IS A PRETTY CRAZY IDEA TO GO WAY OUT THERE FOR A VACATION.......... ....BUT.......WELL...........MAYBE IT'S NOT SO CRAZY AFTER ALL..........

While this example may seem simple or superficial, the basic principles seen here apply in a wide variety of situations. Their true validity, however, will only be understood through trial and error in life situations.

SUMMARY EXAMPLE #2: **AT WORK**

> I'M GLAD YOU'RE COMING TO WORK FOR US. I'VE ALWAYS BELIEVED THAT A PERSON SHOULD BE HIRED BECAUSE OF HIS ABILITY, AND NOT BY THE COLOR OF HIS SKIN, OR HIS RACE. IT DOESN'T BOTHER ME AT ALL! NOT A BIT! NOT A BIT!

> UH! OH!

> YES SIR! I'M GLAD YOU'RE HERE! I BELIEVE IN PROMOTING BROTHERHOOD!

1. *Realizing all emotions are acceptable.*

> HERE I AM AT A NEW JOB, AND INSTEAD OF BEING GLAD, I'M ANGRY!....I SHOULDN'T FEEL THIS WAY....NO! IT HAPPENS I DO FEEL THIS WAY....SOMEPLACE IN ME THIS ANGER MAKES SENSE.....AND IT'S ALL RIGHT FOR ME TO HAVE THESE FEELINGS!

2. *Trusting — Making a conscious effort to withhold judgment.*

> YOU AND YOUR SUPERIOR ATTITUDE! IF YOU'D JUST BE HONEST ABOUT THE WAY YOU FEEL, IT WOULD BE A LOT EASIER!.....I DON'T THINK YOU EVEN SEE YOUR OWN PREJUDICE.....I'VE GOT TO REMEMBER THAT!......HE MAY NOT REALLY KNOW WHAT HE'S DOING..... THAT'S HARD TO BELIEVE....BUT I GUESS I CAN AT LEAST WAIT AND SEE!

> YEAH, I REALLY WANT TO HELP YOU PEOPLE!

3. *Listening — Trying to hear the other's emotional viewpoint.*

> I THINK HE REALLY BELIEVES THAT HIMSELF—THAT HE'S TRYING TO BE HELPFUL....HE MAY BE SINCERE, EVEN IF HE IS INSENSITIVE....I'LL TELL HIM WHAT I HEAR HIM SAYING...

4. Clarifying — Demonstrating our willingness to hear by making clear what feelings have been heard before discussing the "facts."

I HEAR YOU SAYING THAT YOU WANT TO HELP PEOPLE LIKE ME.

IS THAT WHAT I SAID?

DID I REALLY SAY THAT?.... I GUESS I DID....HE MUST THINK I'M AWFULLY ARROGANT....THIS SITUATION IS MAKING ME ANXIOUS ....I WANT IT TO GO WELL.... I CAN TELL HE'S ANXIOUS TOO, EVEN THOUGH I HARDLY KNOW HIM.... WE SHOULDN'T FEEL THIS WAY.... WHAT DO I MEAN WE SHOULDN'T FEEL THIS WAY? WE DO....AT LEAST I DO, AND I'D BETTER ACCEPT IT

An attempt to accept *his* emotions.

I THOUGHT THAT'S WHAT YOU SAID.

I GUESS THAT SOUNDED PRETTY ARROGANT. MAYBE WE'RE BOTH A LITTLE UP TIGHT.

I GUESS WE ARE BOTH A LITTLE UNEASY!

MAYBE HE REALLY HAS SOME SENSITIVITY AFTER ALL.

Even in a situation in which each person is consciously trying to promote a good relationship, inevitably conditions will arise in which the two people disagree. When disagreement occurs, childhood emotions and habits of relating may come to the surface and center around a particular issue. The intensity of these emotions may become far greater than is appropriate to the actual problem.

While this sounds like "information," it is really an attack. The speaker infers "you're irresponsible," yet nothing has been said here to indicate this.

WHY CAN'T JOE DO IT?

JOE IS STILL WORKING ON THAT OTHER PROJECT.

YEAH, I'LL BET HE IS!

WHO'S HE KIDDING! I'M JUST NOT HIS KIND OF PEOPLE!...AND I WAS BEGINNING TO TRUST HIM!...HE WOULDN'T TREAT ANYONE ELSE LIKE THIS!

IF YOU'RE NOT WILLING TO WORK LATE SOMETIMES, MAYBE WE'D BETTER FIND SOMEONE WHO CAN.

I WAS BEGINNING TO TRUST HIM.... I SHOULD HAVE KNOWN. HIS KIND ARE ALL ALIKE! THEY WANT ALL THE ADVANTAGES BUT AREN'T WILLING TO WORK FOR IT.

IF THAT'S THE WAY YOU FEEL, MAYBE YOU'D BETTER FIND SOMEONE ELSE!

At this point, months of growing trust may be swept away because of an automatic childhood response on the part of each person.

On the other hand, if *either* person is adult enough to see the future implications of this moment and act responsibly, a transition might be made to a more mature relationship. (One definition of maturity is "The ability to keep from satisfying an immediate need for the sake of a future goal.")
The atmosphere will change if *either* person can look beyond the childish response of the moment, and make a conscious effort to listen to the other.

YOU FEEL I SHOULD HAVE KNOWN HOW IMPORTANT THIS WAS TO YOU, AND PLANNED TO STAY LATE TONIGHT.

YOU'VE GOT TO LEARN THAT WHEN YOU HAVE A JOB LIKE THIS, YOU'VE GOT TO TAKE RESPONSIBILITY.

He's coming across as a "parent" here.

I HEAR YOU SAYING THAT I HAVEN'T LEARNED TO TAKE RESPONSIBILITY.

WELL......NOT ENTIRELY...I JUST CAN'T BELIEVE YOU'D DO THIS TO ME!

YOU THOUGHT YOU COULD TRUST ME, AND NOW IT SEEMS YOU CAN'T.

YES!

While the problem is far from being solved, the atmosphere has already begun to change . . . preparing a way for a relationship where a solution is possible. But more listening would be helpful. The listener too has a need to be heard, and a better solution is possible if he can know that his emotions are also understood before going further.

Which person listens first is rather unimportant.
A similar improvement in the relationship would
also occur if listening began with the other person.

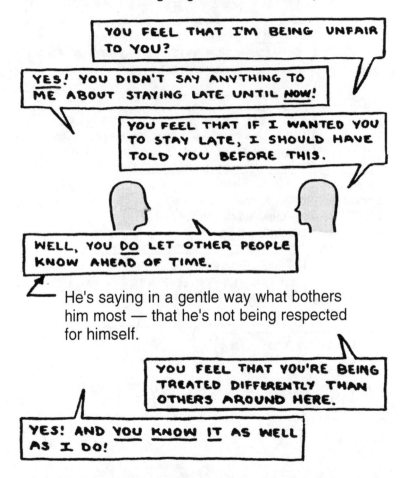

YOU FEEL THAT I'M BEING UNFAIR TO YOU?

YES! YOU DIDN'T SAY ANYTHING TO ME ABOUT STAYING LATE UNTIL NOW!

YOU FEEL THAT IF I WANTED YOU TO STAY LATE, I SHOULD HAVE TOLD YOU BEFORE THIS.

WELL, YOU DO LET OTHER PEOPLE KNOW AHEAD OF TIME.

He's saying in a gentle way what bothers
him most — that he's not being respected
for himself.

YOU FEEL THAT YOU'RE BEING TREATED DIFFERENTLY THAN OTHERS AROUND HERE.

YES! AND YOU KNOW IT AS WELL AS I DO!

The most common response of a listener at
this point is to "explain," but more listening first
will be far more helpful.

Again, the problem has not been solved, but an "openness" has begun which provides an atmosphere in which the problem has the possibility of being worked through.

5. Defining — Clarifying our own territory by making emotions known.

> I STILL FEEL I HAVE A RIGHT TO KNOW AHEAD OF TIME IF I HAVE TO WORK LATE, SO THAT I CAN PLAN ON IT.

> WELL, WE CAN'T BOTHER ABOUT THAT NOW. YOU'LL HAVE TO STAY LATE, AND THAT'S IT.

He is so emotionally involved in getting something done, he isn't hearing him, and doesn't even acknowledge the fact that the request is a reasonable one.

6. Defending — Protecting our own territory by quietly stating choices and taking appropriate action.

> I KNOW HOW IMPORTANT THIS IS TO YOU, AND I'D LIKE TO HELP YOU, BUT I HAVE A VERY IMPORTANT APPOINTMENT MYSELF. ...... IF WE CAN WORK OUT SOME OTHER WAY OF DOING IT. I'LL DO WHAT I CAN. IF YOU INSIST ON MY STAYING LATE TONIGHT THOUGH, I FEEL SO STRONGLY ABOUT THIS THAT I WILL START LOOKING FOR ANOTHER JOB.

Informing the other of his plan of action is also risking of the relationship.

I GUESS WE BOTH FEEL VERY STRONGLY ABOUT THIS. I DON'T WANT YOU TO LEAVE, BUT ON THE OTHER HAND IF YOU DON'T STAY LATE AND HELP WITH THIS IT'S GOING TO CREATE A LOT OF PROBLEMS FOR ME.

I KNOW YOU'RE ON THE SPOT AND I'D LIKE TO HELP, BUT IT'S REALLY VERY IMPORTANT FOR ME TO LEAVE ON TIME TONIGHT. I WISH I COULD HELP.

While nothing has been solved in regard to the problem, the openness that has occurred here has reached a point where practical solutions can be considered.

7. *Exploring alternatives — Examining solutions with self respect.*

I WONDER IF THIS COULD BE SOLVED IN SOME OTHER WAY.

WHAT DO YOU HAVE IN MIND?

NOTHING EXACTLY. IT JUST SEEMS THAT IT MIGHT HELP IF WE TOOK A SECOND LOOK AT THE PROBLEM.

I'D LIKE TO HELP, BUT....

LET'S THINK ABOUT THIS SOME MORE... LET'S SEE.... WHAT IS IT THAT WE ARE TRYING TO SOLVE?.... THIS IS DUE TOMORROW AT TEN AND YOU HAVE TO LEAVE..........

I WONDER IF WE'RE NOT MORE CONCERNED ABOUT A PARTICULAR SOLUTION THAN WHAT NEEDS TO BE DONE....

WHAT DO YOU MEAN?

WELL, WHEN YOU SAID "WHAT ARE WE TRYING TO SOLVE?" I REALIZED THAT THE REAL ISSUE IS NOT WHETHER I STAY LATE OR NOT, BUT GETTING THIS DONE BY TEN TOMORROW

AND......?

IF THE REAL PROBLEM IS GETTING THIS DONE BY TEN, I'D BE WILLING TO COME IN VERY EARLY TOMORROW MORNING AND FINISH IT THEN.

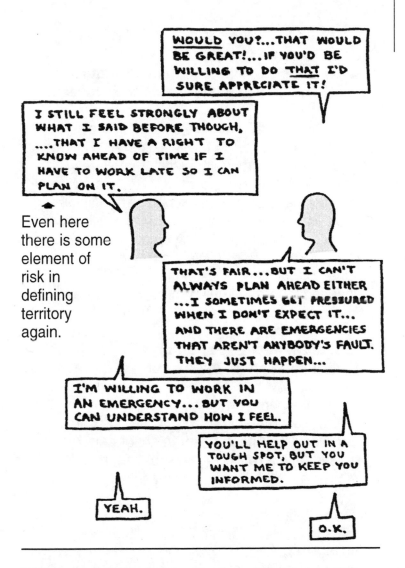

Even here there is some element of risk in defining territory again.

While other differences will arise after this incident, future problems will be more easily solved because of this creative relationship.

FREQUENTLY ASKED QUESTIONS

1. How effective is this method of relating if only one person understands the process?

One person can create a change in the relationship by being the first listener. Through that listening, gradually a shift in attitude will occur in the other person. After this is sensed, the listener can request to be heard as well: "I've listened to you for a while, now will you feed back what you hear me saying? Then I'll listen to you again." If interruptions occur (they probably will!), listening again may be needed before repeating the above request.

2. Suppose, after each person has fully heard the other, there is still a strong disagreement?

Then, the person with the least amount of pain gives to the other. This is not the same as silently "giving in." It is an act of generosity, based on the reality of the situation, and a concern for the other person as well as ourselves.

To measure the depth of the problem for each person is often difficult. Practically, it may be useful to ask each other, "On a scale of 1 to 10, how high is the pain you feel in this situation?" This may help in making a decision.
However, if only one person is repeatedly and

continually feeling the greater pain, it may be necessary to reevaluate the situation, and even the relationship itself.

3. Doesn't defining and defending our territory create problems in a relationship?

Yes. That's usually the reason we avoid speaking up. Yet, remaining silent can cause underground resentment, which ultimately weakens the foundation of the relationship itself. (Resentment is equal to the time we allow a person over our "ouch!" line without saying anything.) While expressing ourselves may cause temporary problems, it is part of the reality of life, and because it is based in our own self worth, it just can't be completely ignored. Problems created by speaking up can usually be resolved by alternately listening to each other, each person clarifying for about five minutes before reversing the process.

We may hesitate to express small ouches ("It's so minor, it doesn't matter"). Yet, speaking up about them ("I'm somewhat bothered by . . .") will probably produce only minor responses. Small ouches that are continually held in, however, can build up, and later cause a sudden explosion.

Many difficulties in relationships could be avoided by each person agreeing on a basic rule: "I'll take responsibility for my 'ouch!' line. If I don't speak up, you can assume all is well between us."

4. How can I reflect back another person's feelings if the other person doesn't say what they are, or is not aware of having feelings?

Usually, each person in a disagreement has a feeling about not getting what he or she wants. A good place to begin communication is a phrase such as, "You seem frustrated about something." This can often help lead to an expression of some feelings. If, after our speaking, we just wait silently (Difficult to do!), the other person will sense that we are paying attention, and will find it easier to say more. We then continue reflecting.

5. What are the most common mistakes people make in trying to solve a mutual problem?

Usually there is a tendency to drift into one of two choices in hopes of changing the situation. Each choice seems to make sense when it is chosen, and only later is it seen as creating difficulties. For lack of a better description, these two seemingly useful actions, often taken to "solve" a disagreement, could be described as "Put Downs" and "Give Ins."

Usually a person outside of an argument can see the destructiveness of a "Put Down" far more clearly than the person using it. The person within the relationship may not think through the possible destructive consequences of a "Put Down" to the other person's "self" respect. The person "Putting Down" might even mistakenly assume that once it is shown that he or she is "right," the argument will quickly end, and even bring a respect and admiration to the "winner." The most common responses to "Put Downs," however, are anger and resentment.

Future problems with "Give Ins," too, may not be clearly seen. "Giving In" for "the sake of the relationship" seems like a helpful thing to do. Yet, a continuous giving away of our own "self" can grow into deepening anger.

"Giving," in contrast to "Giving In," means having respect for the "self" of **both** persons.

6. Why are there so many problems between people if "deep within each person there is a basic healthy drive toward what is seen as good and right"?

To understand this, it's very helpful to get clear about the difference between "the basic healthy drive," (the conscience) and "what is seen as good and right,"(personal information).

While the conscience urges us to be faithful to our personal belief system, it's not the source of our original beliefs. A belief system is developed from each person's individual experiences in life. Beliefs come from the meanings we give to those experiences and the conclusions we reach about what is "true."

From my observation, arguments are not usually between people who see themselves as "mean" or "wrong," but instead, it is between persons who each see themselves as the person who is "right" in a situation.

Arguments are often the result of each person being angry because the other person's conscience does not agree with their own. We become more under-standing when we recognize that the other's conscience is responding to that person's past and the meaning that he or she has given to it.

This, then, may seem to say that the conscience isn't of much value. Actually, it is very helpful in moving us toward the highest value we have within out belief system, urging us toward what seems best.

It's important, however, to distinguish between memories of harsh critical voices in our past and "the still small voice" within us moving us toward healthy fulfillment in emotional maturity.

While there may be rare exceptions, "trusting in the basic healthy drive toward what is seen as good and right" is a positive step in most relationships. Unfortunately, it's very easy to drift into comparing another's conscience with our own and reaching negative conclusions about the other person's character.

Arguing to change another's conscience is usually futile. Telling another person that his or her conscience is wrong, instead of being helpful, simply deepens hostility. Providing understanding of how the person feels, however, and then exchanging information, leads to change, insight, and a creative relationship.

7. Does it take much time to learn REFLECTING and PROTECTING?

Fortunately, as with most skills, we don't have to wait until we've perfected the skill before it can be very useful to us. Opportunities to practice REFLECTING come very frequently, often within minutes. Situations that require PROTECTING usually occur less often and, as they may require a change in attitude, it may take longer to learn.

CHECK LIST FOR PROBLEM SOLVING

1. **What** specifically is to be solved?

2. **When** must it be solved?

3. Is it possible to **expand the time available** before a final decision must be made?

4. What are the **limits** within which we must work - those things that probably won't change? (Could any of these limits be changed, though costly?)

5. Has the main **meaning** of the problem for **each person** been made clear?

6. Has holding on to a **particular solution** become more important than what needs to be done?

7. What **resources** are available to solve the problem?

8. Am I remaining open to a **new and unfamiliar solution** to the problem?

9. What is the **next step**?

10. Am I checking **within myself**, emotionally and spiritually, to see if this choice "feels right"?

COMMENTS ON
THE PROBLEM SOLVING CHECKLIST

1. *What* specifically is to be solved?

Vagueness in defining the problem is often an obstacle in solving it.

The more specific we can be, the closer we are to an answer. (When a car stalls, if we can figure out what the problem is . . . [out of gas, battery dead, dirty carburetor, etc.], we have moved a long way toward solving the problem.)

Summarizing the problem in a sentence or two can sometimes be a key factor in moving toward a solution.

The more specific we can be, the closer we are to an answer.

I'D LIKE TO BE HAPPIER

is a vague statement, and not very helpful.

I'M UNHAPPY IN MY WORK BECAUSE I HAVE ALMOST NO CONTACT WITH PEOPLE

is specific, and points the way toward a solution.

In moving toward an answer, after asking what is to be solved, it is also vital to ask:

2. *When* must it be solved?

Knowing when a final decision must be made has a great effect on how we go about solving the problem . . .

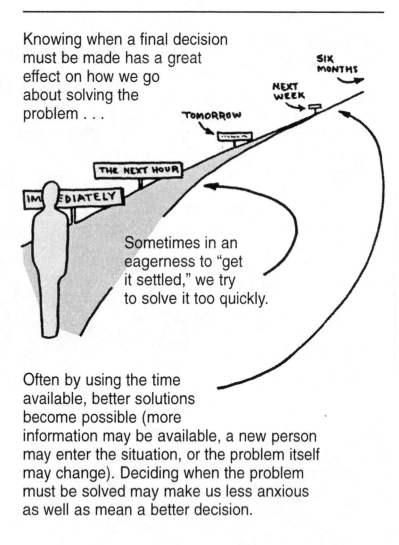

Sometimes in an eagerness to "get it settled," we try to solve it too quickly.

Often by using the time available, better solutions become possible (more information may be available, a new person may enter the situation, or the problem itself may change). Deciding when the problem must be solved may make us less anxious as well as mean a better decision.

Because time is so valuable in solving problems, it is also helpful to ask:

3. Is it possible to *expand the time available* before a final decision must be made?

While delaying a decision is sometimes simply avoiding responsibility, at other times it can be a valuable tool in making a better decision.

An immediate need may cause us to rush into a decision that we may later regret. Sometimes the timo can he expanded by using a temporary solution to meet the immediate ncod.

For Example:

It may be worth the expense to rent a car for a few days instead of buying one in haste simply because we need transportation.

To buy a house in a new community on impulse because "school begins next week" may ultimately be far more costly than temporary lodging.

By examining the reason for the deadline we may find that the problem may be solved on a temporary basis and valuable time for further study can become available to us.

It is also useful to ask:

4.. What are the *limits* within which we must work

While constructive imagination can be hindered by deciding too quickly that "It won't work," ultimately we must face **the limits within which we must function.**

Sometimes problems do not get solved because too much time is spent in day-dreaming about what would happen if this or that were different instead of *facing those limits which probably will not change.*

An architect, in designing a building, is given certain limits within which he must work.

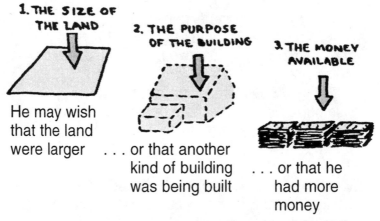

1. THE SIZE OF THE LAND

2. THE PURPOSE OF THE BUILDING

3. THE MONEY AVAILABLE

He may wish that the land were larger   . . . or that another kind of building was being built   . . . or that he had more money

. . . but for practical purposes, his job is to **be as creative as possible within the limits he has been given.**

In every situation we are given certain limits which probably will not change in the near future, such as:

    . . . dealing with a particular person daily.
    . . . living within a limited income.
    . . . living in a certain community.

    . . . having experience in one kind of work.

    . . . having physical limitations.

    . . . living within certain organizational policies.

    . . . etc.

—While it may be possible, through effort and imagination, to ultimately change those limits, *in the meantime our task is to be as creative as possible within the limits we have been given today.*

In "clarifying the limits" we need to ask *what are those factors which probably will not change, within which we have to solve the problem?*

Some specific examples:

WHAT IS OUR MAXIMUM BUDGET FOR THIS?

ARE THERE ORGANIZATIONAL POLICIES WHICH LIMIT US? IF SO WHAT ARE THEY?

DOES LOCATION LIMIT US? IF SO, HOW?

IS HEALTH A FACTOR? IF SO, HOW?

ARE PERSONS LIMITING US? IF SO, IN WHAT WAY?

WHEN MUST THIS BE COMPLETED?

and, a very important question .

ARE THERE LIMITS WHICH COULD BE CHANGED, EVEN IF VERY EXPENSIVE? IS IT POSSIBLY WORTH THE EXPENSE?,

When two or more people are working on a problem, it becomes increasingly important to ask:

5. Has the main *meaning* of the problem for *each person* been made clear?

Every problem had many meanings. For example:

"a home power failure"
may mean

I CAN'T SEE TO FINISH THIS WORK THAT'S DUE TOMORROW, AND I DON'T EVEN HAVE A FLASHLIGHT.

or

I'M GETTING COLD BECAUSE THE FURNACE ISN'T WORKING.

or

I'M GOING TO MISS MY FAVORITE TV SHOW.

While there are many meanings to a problem, some meanings are of more concern than others. It is important to discover the central meaning in any problem we face, because the main meaning we give to a situation determines our actions.

If the *main meaning* of "A HOME POWER FAILURE" is **"I can't see to work"** then our actions will focus on **"finding a temporary light."**

On the other hand, if the *main meaning* of "A HOME POWER FAILURE" is **"I'm getting cold,"** then the focus of our actions will be on *"a way to keep warm."*

While this may seem so obvious that it is hardly worth mentioning, in an actual relationship it may be far from obvious.

Assuming that the other person "should know" what the problem means is a common cause of complications in a relationship.

> WHAT ARE YOU DOING, JUST SITTING THERE? LOOK FOR A FLASHLIGHT!

or

> WHAT ARE YOU DOING UPSTAIRS? I'M FREEZING DOWN HERE, AND YOU DON'T EVEN CARE! YOU KNOW IT'S COLD!

It is vitally important for each person to make clear what the problem means to them.

> I'M WORRIED ABOUT HOW TO GET THAT WORK DONE FOR TOMORROW. I'M GOING TO LOOK FOR A FLASHLIGHT.

> IT'S GETTING REALLY COLD IN HERE! I'VE GOT TO GET SOME BLANKETS.

6. Has holding on to a ***particular solution*** become more important than what needs to be done?

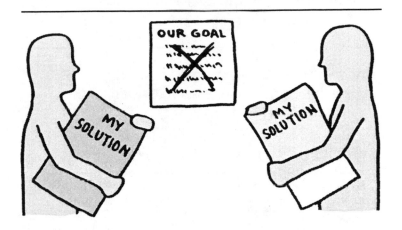

Often a power struggle is not over ***what*** is to be done, but over ***whose method*** will be used.

Parents may, out of false pride, push for their own way at the cost of what is best for the child.

Business associates, in an attempt to win a point may destroy a common purpose.

Husband and wife, by each insisting on certain roles for the other "for the sake of a better relationship" may be preventing the very happiness they both want.

When a struggle over method occurs it is often best to put aside each person's solution, deal with the emotions and begin again to explore alternatives by asking, "What, specifically, is the problem?"

Sometimes, out of pride, we neglect to ask:

7. What *resources* are available to solve
the problem?

Hours of time can be wasted, and work
duplicated, by not making use of information
that is readily available.

We might ask:

> IS THERE ANYONE WHO HAS SOLVED THIS
> PROBLEM, OR A SIMILAR ONE WHO COULD HELP?

> HOW COULD I GET INFORMATION ABOUT
> PEOPLE WHO MIGHT HELP?

> WHERE IS PRINTED MATERIAL AVAILABLE?

> ARE THERE RECORDS ON FILE THAT WOULD
> BE HELPFUL?

> IS THERE A PLACE I COULD VISIT WHERE
> A SIMILAR PROBLEM HAS BEEN SOLVED?

When we face a problem for which there seems to
be "no answer," one of the most useful things we can
do is explore resources and gather information.

8. Am I remaining open to a *new and unfamiliar solution* to the problem?

Because experiences from our past greatly influence what we see and do not see, we tend to use those solutions which fit our pattern of thinking and neglect the unfamiliar.

To allow ourselves to really see something from another's viewpoint,

by
Trusting,
Listening,
and
Clarifying

We may open the way to a new, creative answer to a problem.

Unfortunately, the fear that the other person's viewpoint might *change us* or make us *feel like a child* may keep us from hearing.

yet, **TO BE WILLING TO HEAR ANOTHER'S VIEWPOINT, IS TO ACT CREATIVELY.**

To let go of the familiar is the way to creativity.

Questions encourage imagination:

WHAT WOULD HAPPEN IF WE DID NOTHING?

OR DID IT THE OPPOSITE WAY?

OR TOOK AWAY SOMETHING?

OR ADDED SOMETHING?

OR CHANGED THE TIME? OR PLACE? OR SIZE?

Questions such as these may be explored with someone else or thought through individually for discussion later.

The questions will vary according to the specific problem. Almost every question is helpful if it causes us to see that which is familiar from a fresh perspective.

9. What is the *next step*?

Instead of waiting for "the final solution" before action is taken, it may be helpful, *if one step is clear to TAKE that one step.* The present solution does not have to be the final solution.

Most of us, in solving problems, want a searchlight available which will clearly show us the way, and our final destination . . .

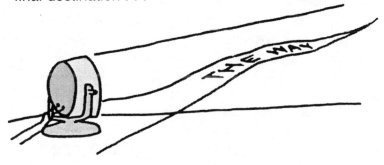

Yet, when we want a "final" answer immediately most problems become overwhelming to us:

"What career is best for me?"

*"How can I live with this person
  30 more years?"*

"What will I do if I'm pregnant?"

"How can I handle an alcoholic problem?"

In reality, living is something like walking with a flashlight in which all we can see is **the next step . . .**

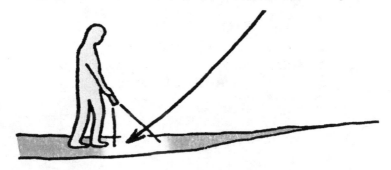

. . . which is all we need to see, for once we have taken that one step, we and the flashlight move forward and the next step can be seen.

In deciding on a career there are small steps which **are** clear possibilities, that could be taken . . . finding an area of general interest and talking with people about it . . . or reading about it . . . or even trying to get a non-skilled job in an area to observe a career close hand.. . . once a step is taken, more light is available for the **next** step.

In deciding what to do about living with a difficult person there are steps that could be taken . . . (Trusting, Listening, and Clarifying is a good beginning!) . . . another is seeking counseling . . . or asking questions and exploring possibilities — what would happen if we separated? . . . Where would each go? . . . What is available? . . . etc.

In exploring what to do about a problem pregnancy . . . the first clear step might be to explore if the pregnancy exists . . . if so, are there agencies available to help me? How and when could I find out more? . . . Is there anyone I could talk with about it? When? . . . etc.

. . . the point here is to ***begin*** solving the problem, by at least getting information, so that the best choice can ultimately be made.

In facing alcoholic problems, simple, quick, and easy solutions are seldom possible. To meet with those who have experience and practical suggestions, however, ***is*** possible. To visit a meeting of Alcoholics Anonymous, or a meeting of their Al-Anon, (to learn how to live with a problem drinker), is one way of beginning. Most phone books list Alcoholics Anonymous. A ***first step*** could be to dial the phone number and ask about it.

Instead of waiting for the "final solution," if one step is ***clear***, we ***can*** take that one step.

10. Am I checking *within myself*, emotionally and spiritually, to see if this choice "feels right"?

While it's vital to think through the various choices before us, paying attention within ourselves can also shed light on our decision.

There is an understanding within us that can reach into our being at a deeper level than logic alone.

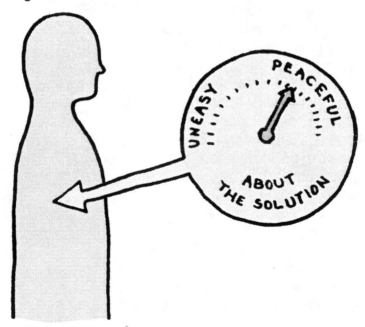

Listening for that inner response, along with the responses of others, can sometimes be the key factor in a decision making process.

INDEX

Acknowledgements

I am especially appreciative of the encouragement and help of my family in this publication: especially my wife, Louise Parsons Pietsch, and my son, Jim Pietsch, my daughter, Patti Pietsch.

I would also like to thank others who have provided practical suggestions and support: Patti Breitman, Paul Lovelace, Susan Page, George Prince, Albert Schinazi, Robert Selverstone, Peggy and James Vaughan, and Mark Wise.

For this edition, special thanks are due to Paul Lovelace for his careful and detailed art direction and cover design, and my son Jim, for his thoughtful consultation and practical help.

DATE DUE			
Aug 27			

2010